A WOMAN'S PILGRIMAGE OF FAITH

*A Daily Guide for Prayer
and Spiritual Maturity*

SHEILA CRAGG

CROSSWAY BOOKS • WHEATON, ILLINOIS
A DIVISION OF GOOD NEWS PUBLISHERS

Library of Congress Cataloging-in-Publication Data

Cragg, Sheila, 1938–
    A woman's pilgrimage of faith : a daily guide for prayer and spiritual maturity / Sheila Cragg.
       p.   cm.
    Includes bibliographical references and index.
    ISBN 1-58134-050-8 (alk. paper)
    1. Chritian women—Prayer-books and devotions—English.
2. Suffering—Religious aspects—Christianity. I. Title.
BV4844.C693 1999
242'.643—dc21
                                        98-55706
                                           CIP

15	14	13	12	11	10	09	08	07	06	05	04	03	02	01	00	99
15	14	13	12	11	10	9	8	7	6	5	4	3	2	1		

CONTENTS

ACKNOWLEDGMENTS

*A*s always, my love and gratitude go to my husband, Ron, who continually holds me up in prayer. I appreciate his constant love and support and unwavering faith. For the more than forty-one years of our marriage, he has been "steadfast, immovable, always abounding in the work of the Lord" (1 Cor. 15:58 NKJV).

A special thank you to the many women who were willing to be transparent in sharing their stories for *A Woman's Pilgrimage of Faith*. In order to protect their privacy, I have changed the names of some of them and minor details of their accounts.

I am indebted to the following women who read the manuscript of this book in its roughest form: Judie Frank, Katie Graham, Shirlee Hickey, Edith Hintz, Nancy Hopkins, Muriel Nelson, Linda Rhodes, Deborah Schultz, and Jutti West. Their suggestions for revisions were especially helpful, as was their encouragement.

Pastor Bruce McLain kindly checked the manuscript for theological clarity and loaned me his books, sermon notes, and other valuable materials.

Judie Frank is my faithful friend and prayer partner. She wrote all the poems that appear in this book. The Lord has used her poems to touch hurting hearts and encourage many in their faith.

The staff at Crossway Books have been a joy to work with on all my devotional books. Marvin Padgett has been a great encourager, and I've appreciated his caring phone calls. Lila Bishop, friend and editor, is always right on target as she gives me direction for each book. She has been a kind listener and continually encouraged me with her prayers.

Fred Rudy, Jill Carter, and Jutti West have been especially helpful and supportive. Cindy Kiple beautifully designed all three books and did the cover illustrations. So many other people at Crossway Books have had an equally important part in seeing the devotional books into publication and marketing them. To each I am deeply grateful. Ron and I have been especially touched by their constant prayer support for us during some very trying times.

INTRODUCTION

*H*ave you ever faltered in your faith during heartbreaking trials? You wondered if you could continue on your spiritual journey. Maybe you've walked away from your faith during trying times or wandered in a dry spiritual wasteland searching for God but not finding Him. Have you been spiritually disappointed with yourself—and God? You questioned if you'd ever find your way back to the Lord or if He would ever find you again.

A loss or series of losses can cause us to question our faith and feel overwhelming emotional and spiritual pain. We wonder if God even cares. We struggle with conflicts between what we expect from God and what we actually experience. During trials we don't have the spiritual victory we hear about from books, messages, and the claims of other Christians.

We're hounded by nagging guilt and even shame that our faith isn't strong enough to hold up in suffering. We may struggle with anger, bitterness, depression, and fear.

We spiritually waver, wanting to hang onto our faith one moment, and the next we want to give up. We know we should trust the Lord and release our burdens into His care. But we can't seem to do it, and we don't understand why we just can't get over our pain or why God doesn't do something to relieve us.

If you relate to such spiritual struggles, join me and many other Christians. This pilgrimage of faith is a spiritual quest, a lifelong journey in a single direction to our heavenly destination. But if you're like me, you feel lost at times. You feel as if you're spiritually taking the long way around to get where you belong.

What makes our pilgrimage difficult and sometimes scary is that the road we travel on is perilous. Heartbreaking losses and trials block our pathway and test our faith. Some of us get stuck and can't get past emotional and spiritual roadblocks.

This book was written to help us get over those obstacles and keep us moving forward spiritually. We'll discover how to deal with many different kinds of major losses and trials we or loved ones experience. If you're looking for easy spiritual answers or quick-fix solutions to suffering, you won't find them here. But we'll learn how to keep on our pilgrimage of faith during trials and find the needed spiritual support to work through grief and pain.

In writing *A Woman's Pilgrimage of Faith,* I've used a wide variety of resources, including personal accounts of many women. They graciously shared their stories of loss and how their faith was challenged in suffering.

This book may not be what you need if you haven't suffered a major loss. But it will help you understand what others are experiencing. It can help you learn how to be more compassionate and minister to those who are hurting.

Often we fail to realize the impact suffering has on our faith. The primary purpose of this book is take us through the entire grieving-healing process and the spiritual phases we go through in suffering. Those three phases include spiritual reaction, rebuilding, and renewal.

In the spiritual reaction phase, we can't believe God has allowed us to experience this painful loss. In the spiritual rebuilding phase, we have moved beyond our initial spiritual shock and have started growing in our faith through grief and trials. The spiritual renewal phase brings us into a deeper relationship with our Comforter who is always with us to love and support us in our pain.

A Woman's Pilgrimage of Faith will help us gain an understanding of what we experience spiritually as we're going through trials. We'll discover how we grow through grief and come out with a stronger faith. We'll come to terms with the mysteries of suffering, find spiritual meaning, and see how God can turn our losses into a ministry to other hurting people.

One of my concerns as you work through this healing process is the danger of being defeated by negative self-talk and shame-filled thoughts, such as: *I shouldn't be anxious. I shouldn't hurt so much. I shouldn't cry. I'm dumb or stupid for feeling this way.*

Even the strongest Christians hurt, sin, and have spiritual conflicts. We're all on this pilgrimage of faith, so keep reminding yourself that the Lord accepts you as you are and how you feel. He is always present with you to support you through this healing, spiritually renewing process. I pray you will become more accepting and gentle with yourself as you and the Lord work through this healing process.

One of my greatest desires in writing this book was to encourage you that keeping your faith in suffering has great significance in the eyes of God and an unseen host of witnesses as well. Our losses can have personal and spiritual meaning, and our steadfast trust in the Lord counts for all eternity. I hope you will come to rely on the Lord's ever-loving kindness. He is always with you no matter how dark and deep your heartaches go.

Here are some suggestions to help you use this book. The devotionals don't have to be completed in a week, so give yourself the freedom to work through the book at your own pace.

Each week's opening page has a Scripture passage that can be memorized. This is followed by a chapter and seven days of brief devotional studies on the same subject.

Before you start reading each day's devotional, write the date on the blank line at the top of the page. Later you may want to reread what you've written. The dates will help you relate your written responses to the events and concerns you were experiencing during that period. You will be able to compare where you were in your pilgrimage of faith and how you have progressed since then.

Each day's devotion begins with Scripture passages that correlate with the chapter theme. The "Scripture Reading" and "Practicing the Spiritual Life" were based on the *Holy Bible: New International Version* (NIV). Using this Bible or another modern version will make it easier to answer the questions in that section. You may want to look up passages in several different versions to gain a greater depth of meaning.

Under "Practicing the Spiritual Life," the first question pertains to the "Scripture Reading," and the second set of questions are for personal application. You will also find some assignments to help you work through the grieving-healing process and grow spiritually. Take time to seriously consider those questions, pray, and seek the Lord's guidance. The questions are meant to help you apply the truths of Scripture to your everyday life.

If the personal application questions do not speak to your particular experience, feel free not to answer them. We all respond to losses and grieve in different ways. The questions can help you understand what others may feel or experience during trials.

For those who enjoy keeping a journal, a loose-leaf notebook with plenty of writing paper will be especially helpful. Use the notebook to answer questions from "Practicing the Spiritual Life," adding your own thoughts and feelings.

If you don't enjoy writing, give brief answers. The lined spaces in this book will provide enough writing space. Don't worry about spelling or how well you write. What you put on paper is personal and private, for your spiritual growth and benefit, and is between you and the Lord alone. Above all, He accepts and loves you the way you are and just the way you write.

You may find it helpful to photocopy the "Prayer" and brief sections of this book that speak to your heartfelt needs. Then paste the photocopied information into your notebook or on small file cards. You can carry them with you and refer to them in spare moments. Or color highlight parts of the book that especially minister to you so you can easily find them again.

It helps to read over what you've written in this book and/or your notebook. But as you're reading, don't criticize yourself or dwell on hurtful self-talk. Add more comments only if you need to clarify what you've written. If you constantly put yourself down, you'll defeat yourself and become stuck in past hurts. You need to understand what you're feeling and thinking, so you can get through the grieving process, find necessary healing, and strengthen your faith.

Keep affirming to yourself that the Lord is kind. He loves you so much He desires to heal you of your hurts. He has promised, "I have loved you with an everlasting love; I have drawn you with loving-kindness" (Jer. 31:3).

Finally, the daily devotional studies close with a personalized Scripture prayer. Those prayers will help you present your needs to the Lord, confess sin, comfort your heart, and find healing. *A Woman's Pilgrimage of Faith* concludes with a spiritual retreat and a Remembrance Ceremony to help you find closure and to affirm life-changing experiences. This is followed by "Remembrance Ceremony Readings" and "Plans for a Small Group Study and Spiritual Retreat."

It is my prayer that as you use this book, you may grow through grief and discover the joy of having your faith refined and renewed. "In this you greatly rejoice, though now for a little while you may have had to suffer grief in all kinds of trials. These have come so that your faith—of greater worth than gold, which perishes even though refined by fire—may be proved genuine and may result in praise, glory and honor when Jesus Christ is revealed" (1 Peter 1:6-7).

W E E K   O N E

Storm-Tossed Faith

"If any of you lacks wisdom, let him ask God,
who gives to all men generously
and without reproaching,
and it will be given him.
But let him ask in faith, with no doubting,
for he who doubts is like a wave of the sea
that is driven and tossed by the wind."

JAMES 1:5-6 RSV

*W*e were spending our fortieth wedding anniversary in the village of Cambria on the central coast of California. As my husband, Ron, rested in the motel room after a long drive, I sat on a rough-hewn bench on the cliffs overlooking Moonstone Beach. My exhaustion lifted, and my soul was refreshed as I gazed at the silken blue sky, vast tranquil sea, and majestic Monterey pines gracing the rugged coastline.

It was as bright as daylight that Friday evening at 8:00 P.M. Surfers in black wet suits perched on their surfboards waiting to ride the ocean's waves, but the placid breakers rolled lazily ashore. The gentle whitewashed surf was fringed in lacy foam—quite a contrast to the savage sea storms that had at one time uprooted giant trees and tossed them along the shore.

I worked my way down the steep earthen steps to the rock-strewn beach. I combed through wet rocks until I found a small heart-shaped stone to add to my collection. The rust and sand-gray heart was pierced with three pin-sized holes. Then I discovered a white misshapen heart stone with an ingrained gray ribbon across it.

I was fascinated by the varied colors and shapes of the stones—eggs, flats, oblongs, ovals, and rounds. Some pebbles looked like shiny chocolate-covered candies. Many rocks had a polished sheen, others a rough sandy finish.

Gemstone Faith

The sea-smoothed stones reminded me of how our faith can be turned from a jagged rock into a gem. The ocean, a giant gemstone tumbler, turns stones end over end, washing them up and down the shore. The constant rolling motion of waves grinds rocks and sand together, smoothing sharp-edged stones through abrasion.

Life's rock tumbler rough-grinds our faith through the abrasion of trials and gritty everyday irritations. Constant waves of suffering can turn us end over end, tossing us from one crisis to the next until we feel as if our heart is pierced with sorrow.

Rocks that are used for polishing must possess certain qualities; one of them is hardness. On the hardness scale, our skin is about 1.5 compared to a diamond's 10, which is thousands of times harder. Our faith needs to have the durability and hardness to hold up under abrasive, grinding pressures if it's going to have diamond-like quality.

On the surface, a polished rock may appear to be a gemstone, but closer examination reveals nearly invisible defects and fractures. We may outwardly display spiritual strength until sharp blows break us open, exposing defects in our faith.

Some rocks are broken into fragments; then a piece is cut into the shape of a gem and tumbled with abrasives to grind away sharp edges. Before the Lord is able to begin preparing us for the gem-making process, we may feel as if we've been broken and splintered into pieces.

To hurry any part of the lengthy grinding-polishing process will produce an inferior gemstone, and so it is with our faith. Our trust in God can be turned into a gem if we're willing to endure the grinding, shaping, tumbling, sanding, and polishing process. To develop a commitment to Christ of the highest quality, we need to be willing to submit to this lifelong faith-transforming process.

Hammering trials break off the rough edges of sin, and grinding hardships chip away superficial spirituality. Heart-tumbling losses deepen and strengthen our faith; sorrows form and shape compassion; painful sanding makes us spiritually tender, and tedious time-consuming polishing turns us into Christ-glorifying gemstones.

But are we willing to surrender ourselves to the Master stonecutter so He can grind and polish and shape us into His image?

Storm-Tossed Faith

During the past three months our family has been through a series of faith-testing trials. Ron's brother collapsed in his apartment, and it was two days before he could reach the phone to call for help. He was rushed to the hospital with congestive heart failure. Ron also had blood tests showing the possibility of cancer, and he was scheduled for more tests.

Our area was struck by massive flooding, mud slides, and highway washouts. Our son and his wife had just moved into their first home, and one end was flooded, ruining new carpet. Ron sells auto parts along the central coast of California and kept getting caught in blinding rainstorms.

Both cars and computers kept breaking down. I lost more than fifty hours of work due to crashing computers. The mechanical failures were fixable. But on and on it went with many other heartbreaking concerns that were not fixable.

On the morning of March 31, I was feeling relieved. Ron's tests for cancer had come out negative. His brother had recovered, and other problems had been resolved.

But at the doctor's office that day, I was shocked when he told me a minor rash on my back was the shingles, which soon made me terribly sick. Then Ron's car broke down again. My sister was rushed to the emergency room; she had her fifth diabetic coma in four months. That night I was again wondering if we'd ever see relief.

The apostle Peter says, "Dear friends, do not be surprised at the painful trial you are suffering, as though something strange were happening to you. But rejoice that you participate in the sufferings of Christ, so that you may be overjoyed when his glory is revealed" (1 Peter 4:12-13).

But I am surprised by trying ordeals. Here I am writing about keeping our faith in suffering and having to live through what I write about. To share in Christ's suffering sounds courageous until I experience trials, and then I wonder why the Lord allows them.

Christ calls us to glorify Him whether we suffer personal affliction or persecution for His sake. But how could I glorify the Lord when I so easily gave way to self-pity and felt spiritually weak? How could the Lord use me to minister to others when my trust in Him was filled with defects and flaws?

I knew the Lord didn't find fault with me for asking for His help and wisdom to deal with trials. Yet He said I must ask in faith without hesitation or doubting. But my feelings were like surges of sea waves driven by the wind. While I was tossing to and fro between all sorts of questions and conflicting emotions, the Lord couldn't give me the guidance I so desperately needed (James 1:5-7).

As I read the Matthew passage about the disciples in a storm at sea, I related to their fears. Didn't Jesus realize that suffering whips up furious storms of uncertainty? He was sleeping, and the winds were rising and raging around me also, and waves of anxiety and fear were sweeping over me. I was struggling to steer the boat and make it safely to shore. The harder I fought to stay in control, the more I sank into the depths, until I felt like crying out, "Wake up, Lord; save me! I'm going to drown!"

"You of little faith, why are you so afraid?" (Matt. 8:26a). Jesus' sharp answer to His disciples and to me shocked me; it seemed so harsh. Then I realized that He was right to reprove me; my faith was small. As I fixed my eyes on Him and took them off the turbulent storms, I was amazed by the miracle He performed. He rebuked winds and waves of turmoil and soothed my battered spirit with His calming peace.

Enduring Faith

Affliction is a natural though painful part of our lives. We're broken people in a broken world. Grievous trials are common to all adults and children around the world, millions of whom live and die in the despair of poverty and starvation.

Suffering is guaranteed because of our human condition. We were born in sin. Yet when we suffer, we may question why God let tragedy happen to us. Where is He? Or we may blame those who have wounded us. Or we ask, "What have I done so terribly wrong that I'm suffering such unbearable pain?"

So how do we have faith that will endure in tough times? As painful as our trials may be, they can "turn out to be the most important opportunity we are ever going to have to honestly love God and truly trust Him in a way which will bring Him joy and defeat Satan."[1] We defeat Satan by resisting him, standing firm in our faith and growing spiritually stronger in suffering (1 Peter 5:8-9).

For example, Satan accused God of making Job happy and wealthy and protecting his home and property. But Job maintained his spiritual integrity, continued to fear God, and had nothing to do with evil even though his ten children and servants were killed, and he lost everything. Job "did not sin by charging God with wrongdoing" (Job 1:22b).

When God pointed out to Satan that Job still feared Him even though Satan had harmed Job without cause, "Satan replied to the Lord, 'Skin for skin—he blesses you only because you bless him. A man will give up everything he has to save his life. But take away his health, and he will surely curse you to your face!'" (Job 2:4-5 NLT). Even after Job lost his health and his wife's respect, he proved that Satan's accusations against him were wrong. Job still held onto his faith in the Lord.

We are faced with the same challenge today. Will we trust the Lord and maintain spiritual integrity in suffering? Or will we accuse the Lord of wrong-doing, turn away from Him, and try to run away from our trials?

We cannot escape losses and hardships, no matter how hard we try. "Loss is like a terminal illness. There is nothing we can do to spare ourselves from such sickness, except perhaps put it off for a while."[2] But in our affliction the Lord can heal us from another sickness, which is a diseased faith and "the sickness of our souls. . . . If we face loss squarely and respond to it wisely, we will actually become healthier people, even as we draw closer to physical death. We will find our souls healed, as they can only be healed through suffering."[3]

Though we may be emotionally and physically weakened by heartaches, our spiritual lives can be strengthened. When we suffer a loss, the only thing we may have control over is our attitude and how we respond spiritually.

"It is not, therefore, the *experience* of loss that becomes the defining moment of our lives, for that is as inevitable as death, which is the last loss awaiting us all. It is how we *respond* to loss that matters. That response will largely determine the quality, the direction, and the impact of our lives."[4]

This is our hope in sorrow. Our souls can be healed and our faith transformed as we experience the power of the Lord's redeeming grace in the midst of affliction.

Spiritual Reaction, Rebuilding, and Renewal Phases

The purpose of this devotional book is to help us learn how to keep trusting the Lord during affliction. The goal is to discover spiritual meaning in trials and strengthen our commitment to Christ. The reaction, rebuilding, and renewal phases that we may experience during suffering will be identified in order to help us understand the faith-testing process.

When we encounter suffering, initially we experience a range of emotions that is termed the *spiritual reaction phase*. We may be stunned by disbelief, shocked, and stricken with grief at the painful loss God has allowed us to experience. We may have a crisis of faith or question our beliefs about a caring heavenly Father.

At this critical turning point, we make certain decisions. We may determine to grow spiritually stronger in our afflictions. We may become stuck in spiritual bitterness, or we are unable to accept our suffering, and we blame the Lord for it. Or we turn away from the Lord because we're so hurt and disappointed with Him.

If we determine to grow spiritually through the affliction, we move into the *spiritual rebuilding phase*. We relinquish control of our life to the Lord. We let go of our expectations about what the Lord and others should do and release our burdens and heartaches into His care. We realize that our lives have been permanently changed by our loss, and we cannot return to life the way it was before.

We begin the spiritual rebuilding process as we search for and discover spiritual meaning. Thus we find hope as the Lord enables us to release hurtful situations into His care. We grow spiritually through our grief.

Third, during the *spiritual renewal phase*, our faith is perfected, and we experience deeper levels of spiritual maturity. We realize that our commitment to the Lord in tough times has eternal significance, and we see how He can use our trials for His glory.

The Lord becomes our unlimited source of strength in weakness as we are comforted by His ever-caring presence and constant support. Out of our own suffering, we accept Christ's call to become compassionate servants and comfort others so they, too, may find healing and spiritual renewal.

As we work through the spiritual reaction, rebuilding, and renewal phases, may we come to possess enduring faith, abiding hope, and everlasting love for our Lord. May God-given peace be our anchor. May the grace and mercy of our Savior be our surety. May our faith be turned into a precious gemstone of unsurpassed value.

Scripture Reading: Matthew 8:23-27

Practicing the Spiritual Life

How did the disciples react when they felt their lives were being threatened?

_____

_____

What stormy trials would you like to see Jesus bring to a complete calm?

_____

_____

For what concerns do you need to have greater faith and less fear?

_____

_____

Prayer

"The mighty oceans have roared, O Lord. The mighty oceans roar like thunder; the mighty oceans roar as they pound the shore." "You have thrust me down to the lowest pit, into the darkest depths. Your anger lies heavy on me; wave after wave engulfs me." "Your waves and surging tides sweep over me." I reel and stagger like a drunken person; I am at my wits' end. I cry out to You, Lord, in my trouble; bring me out of my distress. O still the storm to a whisper; the waves of the sea to a hush. For mightier than the violent raging of the seas, mightier than the breakers on the shore, O Lord, You are mightier than these! (Ps. 93:3 NLT; Ps. 88:6-7 NLT; Ps. 42:7b NLT not paraphrased; Ps. 107:27-29; Ps. 93:4 NLT paraphrased)

Prayers, Praises, and Personal Notes

_____

_____

_____

Scripture Reading: James 1:5-6

Practicing the Spiritual Life

When we ask for wisdom during trials, what does God promise He will do?

_____

_____

In what areas are you struggling with doubts and/or wavering in your faith?

_____

_____

Every day this week write down how the Lord gave you wisdom to deal with a trying situation.

_____

_____

Prayer

O Risen Savior, as You asked Your disciples, You are also asking me, "Why are you troubled, and why do doubts rise in your minds?" Lord, "I do believe; help me overcome my unbelief!" "Increase my faith!" Then I will not waver through unbelief regarding Your promises, God, but I will be strengthened in my faith and give glory to You, being fully persuaded that You have the power to do what You have promised. Now teach me to number my days aright that I may gain a heart of wisdom. Guide me in the way of wisdom and lead me along straight paths. (Luke 24:38; Mark 9:24b paraphrased; Luke 17:5b not paraphrased; Rom. 4:20-21; Ps. 90:12; Prov. 4:11 paraphrased)

Prayers, Praises, and Personal Notes

_____

_____

_____

Scripture Reading: 1 Peter 4:12-13

Practicing the Spiritual Life

What should not surprise us or seem strange?

_____

_____

What trials have surprised you and made you think something unfair or unusual was happening to you?

_____

_____

How would you like to bring glory and honor to the Lord in your trials?

_____

_____

Prayer

O my Hope, my Savior in times of distress, why are You like a stranger in the land, like a traveler who stays only a night? Why are You like a man taken by surprise, like a warrior powerless to save? You are with me, O Lord, and I bear Your name; do not forsake me! Now if I am Your child, then I am an heir—Your heir, O God, and co-heirs with You, Jesus, if indeed I share in Your sufferings in order that I may also share in Your glory. I consider that my present sufferings are not worth comparing with the glory that will be revealed in me. I glory in Your holy name; my heart seeks You, Lord, and rejoices. (Jer. 14:8-9; Rom. 8:17-18; Ps. 105:3, all paraphrased)

Prayers, Praises, and Personal Notes

_____

_____

_____

Scripture Reading: Hebrews 12:2-3

Practicing the Spiritual Life
For what did Jesus endure the cross and a shameful death?

_____

_____

When we undergo suffering, what do we need to consider?

_____

_____

For what heartaches do you need to fix your eyes on Jesus?

_____

_____

Prayer
Jesus, You emptied Yourself, taking the form of a slave, being born in human likeness. And being found in human form, You humbled Yourself and became obedient to the point of death—even death on a cross. Therefore I will not lose heart. Though outwardly I am wasting away, yet inwardly I am being renewed day by day. For my light and momentary troubles are achieving for me an eternal glory that far outweighs them all. So I fix my eyes not on what is seen, but on what is unseen. For what is seen is temporary, but what is unseen is eternal. (Phil. 2:7-8 NRSV; 2 Cor. 4:16-18, all paraphrased)

Prayers, Praises, and Personal Notes

_____

_____

_____

_____

Scripture Reading: Job 1:1-3, 6-12

Practicing the Spiritual Life
What did God say to Satan about Job's character and faith?

_____

_____

What did Satan say about how Job would react to suffering?

_____

_____

What would you like God to say about your character and faith?

_____

_____

Prayer
Lord, I will fear You and shun evil. For Your grace, O God, that brings salvation has appeared to me. It teaches me to say no to ungodliness and worldly passions and to live a self-controlled, upright, and godly life in this present age, while I wait for the blessed hope—Your glorious appearing, my great God and Savior, Jesus Christ. May You, O God, the God of peace, sanctify me through and through. May my whole spirit, soul, and body be kept blameless at Your coming, Lord Jesus Christ. (Prov. 3:7b; Titus 2:11-13; 1 Thess. 5:23, all paraphrased)

Prayers, Praises, and Personal Notes

_____

_____

_____

Scripture Reading: Job 1:13-22

Practicing the Spiritual Life

How did Job react to the loss of his children, servants, and all his possessions?

_____

_____

_____

How can Job's response to suffering help you through your own?

_____

_____

_____

Prayer

O Lord, I bow down in worship; I kneel before You. For as I came from my mother's womb, I shall go again, naked as I came, and shall take nothing for my labor, which I may carry away in my hand. This also is a grievous evil: Just as I came, so shall I go; and what gain have I? I have labored for the wind. But I am confident, Lord, that everything You do will endure forever; nothing can be added to it, and nothing taken from it—so that I may revere You. "What is more, I consider everything a loss compared to the surpassing greatness of knowing Christ Jesus my Lord, for whose sake I have lost all things. I consider them rubbish, that I may gain Christ." (Ps. 95:6; Eccl. 5:15-16 RSV; Eccl. 3:14 paraphrased; Phil. 3:8 not paraphrased)

Prayers, Praises, and Personal Notes

_____

_____

_____

Scripture Reading: Job 2:1-10

Practicing the Spiritual Life

What did God say to Satan about Job after he'd lost his children, servants, and everything he owned?

_____

_____

How did Job respond when he was afflicted with painful sores?

_____

_____

Throughout the day make a list of the ways you see God's goodness.

_____

_____

Prayer

Father God, "we looked for peace, but no good came; and for a time of health, and behold trouble!" You are good, O my Fortress, a stronghold in the day of trouble; and You know me, for I trust in You. Therefore, it's better that I am poor and walk in my integrity, than dishonest, perverse in speech, and a fool. "May integrity and uprightness protect me, because my hope is in you." "I will praise you forever for what you have done; in your name I will hope, for your name is good. I will praise you in the presence of your saints." (Jer. 8:15 KJV not paraphrased; Nahum 1:7 KJV; Prov. 19:1 KJV paraphrased; Ps. 25:21; 52:9 not paraphrased)

Prayers, Praises, and Personal Notes

_____

_____

_____

WEEK TWO

Shock and Disbelief

*"In my alarm I said,
'I am cut off from your sight!'
Yet you heard my cry for mercy
when I called to you for help."*

PSALM 31:22

*T*en years ago Ron had a coronary angiogram to check for possible blockages. The doctor said he would discuss the results with me in the hospital waiting room. After waiting much longer than the test was supposed to last, I checked with the clerk, who told me the doctor had returned to his office.

When I called the doctor, he snapped, "I didn't think you were at the hospital."

His attitude stunned me and intensified my shock when he told me Ron was at risk for a heart attack, should not leave the hospital, and needed immediate bypass surgery. I was sitting by the pay phone, feeling dazed and disengaged from myself, as if watching the whole scene from a distance. I was so numb I couldn't even cry. Ron was only fifty-two, and I was terrified that he might die.

In Gerald Sittser's book *A Grace Disguised*, he wrote about his shock and tormented feelings after his mother, wife, and four-year-old daughter were killed in an accident. A drunken driver's car going eighty-five miles per hour struck the family's minivan head-on. Sittser described his reaction: "I felt dizzy with grief's vertigo, cut off from family and friends, tormented by the loss, nauseous from the pain. After arriving at the hospital, I paced the floor like a caged animal. . . . I was so bewildered that I was unable to voice questions or think rationally. I felt wild with fear and agitation."[1]

The Impact of Shock

Shock can hit us head-on, impair how we act and think, and assault our emotions as well. We feel as if we're functioning normally, but in reality we do not act or think clearly at all. We are overcome by alarm, confusion, and disorientation. We do not remember essential information and focus instead on unimportant details.

"When we are in shock, our bodies are in a state of severe physiological alarm. This physical response is a natural reaction when our sense of security is threatened. We do not perceive the world as safe any longer, so we set up a defensive reaction that keeps us alert to anything that is unusual or fearful."[2]

Some people collapse emotionally and physically and suffer sudden attacks of fatigue, trembling, and weakness. Others lose their appetite, feel restless, are in a constant state of alert, wanting to sleep but can't. Ordinary tasks they could normally handle become overwhelming.

They seesaw between reality and unreality, aware one moment that tragedy has struck and denying it the next. Painful, powerful forces dictate their lives, and the impact of shock and loss of control is frightening.

Shock can reduce us to silence; we're so stunned we can't speak about our loss or listen to others discussing it. We want them to be quiet and leave us alone. Yet we don't want to be alone. We need comforting, compassionate people around us.

When we hear bad news, we can be so stricken by shock that we can't remember what was said or keep the information straight. Recently Ron had laser surgery on his eye. The surgeon took us through a booklet with pictures as he explained the severity of the deterioration in medical terminology we didn't understand.

I could feel myself going into shock and shutting down. About all I heard was "could lose an eye." I knew we wouldn't recall much of what the surgeon said, so I asked for a copy of the booklet. Later I was able to read about his condition when I was more able to comprehend the information.

Spiritual Shock and Disbelief

During the spiritual reaction phase, people may question their beliefs about God, their relationship with Him, and His role in their suffering. While coping with their loss, they feel as if their trust in God has been struck head-on by a devastating force.

Then, too, disbelief may not descend during the initial stages of a grievous trial. It can strike at any time during or even after the crisis when people cannot accept that a painful loss is permanent and unchangeable in spite of their prayers and the prayers of others.

Cindy shared her experience of struggling with spiritual shock and disbelief after her painful losses. "I was fired from two jobs in a short period of time. I lost the first job after working at a small company for five years. I was shocked because I had a very good relationship with the clients. I knew Hal, the owner, could be a corrupt and vindictive person. He bragged about keeping a former employee from getting another job. I was afraid he'd do the same to me, but I found a temporary job that turned permanent.

"Then I lost that job after a few months because I was unwilling to work sixty to seventy hours a week for forty hours of pay. I was shocked that God would allow this to happen to me again.

"The job I now have is exactly what I'd prayed for, and the Lord continues to confirm that in many ways. It's been two years since I was fired the first time, but I still struggle spiritually with disbelief and feelings of insecurity."

Here are some ways we can experience spiritual shock and disbelief: We may not realize our true condition because we may possess God-given peace. This peace and shock are an anesthetic that numbs the intensity of the pain, which may last for several days or weeks or months before we are assaulted by the full impact of a loss.

On the other hand, we may be in such spiritual turmoil that we have no sense of peace at all. Anxiety so overcomes us that we're unable to trust the Lord. We may not believe that God has allowed us to be stricken by a painful loss. Initially, disbelief can be an insulation that allows us to gradually face our loss. Acute spiritual sorrow would be intolerable without this buffer. Disbelief offers us temporary relief from grim reality.

We may feel as if God has abandoned and forsaken us. We beg God to answer the questions that haunt us, as David pleaded, "My God, my God! Why have you forsaken me? Why do you remain so distant? Why do you ignore my cries for help?" (Ps. 22:1 NLT).

On the cross Jesus cried out in a loud voice, "My God, my God, why have you forsaken me?" (Matt. 27:46). "God as Father did not forsake him; . . . but God as Judge had to be separated from him if he was to experience spiritual death in the place of sinful men."[3] Jesus felt forsaken of His Father as He bore the weight of our sins. We can find comfort that Jesus knows the depth of our grief when we feel forsaken by God.

When people are in spiritual shock, they may have difficulty praying, serving, and worshiping the Lord. They may have a shortened attention span and cannot concentrate when they try to pray, read, or listen to a sermon. They start reading the Bible but become so distracted by their concerns that they don't remember anything they read. They feel so dazed and numb they can't pray, and if they do pray, they don't know what to ask for. How can they pray when nothing makes sense?

They may feel empty when they attend church and come away without remembering anything about the service. They may find it nearly impossible to attend church and/or continue in Christian service. During a worship service when a hymn or a point in the message reminds them of their heartache, they can be overcome with grief. Their own personal and spiritual needs can so overwhelm them that they are unable to comfort others who are hurting.

On the other hand, the stress of the situation may keep people from recognizing when the Lord has answered and intervened. When an angel delivered Peter from prison, he went to the house where Christians were praying for him. Rhoda came to the outer door and recognized Peter's voice. She was so overjoyed and shocked that she didn't let him in but ran to tell the believers. But they didn't believe her. "'You're out of your mind,' they told her. When she kept insisting that it was so, they said, 'It must be his angel'" (Acts 12:15).

Finding Comfort During Spiritual Shock

We need to realize that spiritual shock is a normal response to loss and allow ourselves time to work through it. We can do so by finding a Bible verse that especially comforts our heart. We can read it over and over when we can't concentrate on reading longer passages. We can pray some of the psalms to express our shock and disbelief.

We can affirm our Shepherd's caring presence even when nothing has changed about our heartache. David was transparent about his spiritual distress while affirming the Lord's love and awareness of his anguish. "I will be glad and rejoice in your love, for you saw my affliction and knew the anguish of my soul" (Ps. 31:7).

The Lord has also helped me by providing prayer partners. As we share and pray, the Lord helps us work through our reactions to the crisis. We give each other spiritual insights, permission to feel the way we do, and help each other find balance and perspective.

Ministering to Others in Spiritual Shock

How can we minister to hurting people when they express disbelief, are in spiritual shock, and question why God allows them to go through intense trials? How can we comfort others when they try to pray and cannot feel

God's presence or sense His care? It's important that we do not make them feel guilty about their expressions of disbelief and feelings of distance from the Lord.

When people are in a dazed spiritual condition, they are unable to bear, hear, or receive our advice or the verses we quote. When praying aloud with people in spiritual shock, don't preach at them by "telling God" how they should act or feel. We can silently pray for hurting people that they may experience the assurance of the Lord's unfailing love and support. We need to be sensitive to others in pain by not quoting Scripture in a trite or superior way. Say as little as possible; show the genuineness of your compassion by your quiet gentle caring.

Job's friends did one kind thing for him before they launched their verbal attacks. When they first saw him, they were so horrified by his devastating losses and disfigured condition that they sat in silent sympathy with him for seven days. "They were true friends, bringing to Job's lonely ash-heap the compassion of a silent presence."[4]

We need to sit with people in shock, wait for them to speak, and listen without giving advice. We can hug them, hold them, and weep with them. The most meaningful things we can say are simply: "I love you." "I care for you." Or "I'm holding you up in prayer." We can allow them to guide us as to what they need. We can ask, "How can I best pray for you?"

A hurting person may say, "I don't know what I need," or "I don't know what to pray." Then we can reassure them that we will continue to pray for them and be with them when they need us.

We can send cards that express compassion and offer a comforting promise of the Lord's unfailing love. I've kept cards and notes that have been sent to me when I was struggling with the shock and disbelief of a heartache, and sometimes I read them again for comfort.

Last year I went through a difficult five weeks after my doctor discovered a rash that he said could be cancerous. His alarm and over-concern scared me. Fortunately I did not have cancer, and the rash turned out to be insignificant.

During the weeks before I found out the results of the biopsy, I was in emotional and spiritual shock. This devotional book had just been accepted for publication, and I questioned how I could write this book and deal with cancer at the same time.

But I know many godly friends in ministry who have suffered catastrophic diseases and continued serving the Lord. Sometimes God deepens His work in people by allowing severe suffering. Those friends have encouraged me spiritually as they persevered in pain and maintained their faithfulness to the Lord.

Judie, my prayer partner, suffered from Hodgkin's disease twenty years ago, but after undergoing a difficult regime of treatments, she was cancer free. She empathized with my fear and designed a greeting card that simply said on the front, "Sheila, I'm praying for you." On the inside of the card, she'd written the following poem that helped sustain me through that ordeal because I knew she would be there to comfort and support me whenever I needed her.

I'LL BE THERE

I want you to know I'll be there if the going gets tough.
I'll be there to help you when the day is rough.
You can count on me anytime, anywhere.
Just let me know and I'll be there.
I'll listen to you if you want to talk.
I'll be there, for together this path we'll walk.
I'll hold your hand and spend time with you.
You won't be alone because I'll be there for you.
I'll ask God to encourage you each time I pray.
Remember He'll be there each step of the way.[5]

Scripture Reading: Matthew 27:45-50

Practicing the Spiritual Life

What did Jesus cry out on the cross, and how do you think He felt at that moment?

_____

_____

_____

During what affliction have you experienced Jesus' comfort when others had forsaken you?

_____

_____

_____

Prayer

"My God, my God, why have you forsaken me? Why are you so far from saving me, so far from the words of my groaning?" "Let me not be put to shame, O Lord, for I have cried out to you; but let the wicked be put to shame and lie silent in the grave." "Do not forsake me, O Lord; O my God, be not far from me!" "Draw near to me, redeem me, set me free." "I trust in you, O Lord; I say, 'You are my God.'" (Ps. 22:1; Ps. 31:17; Ps. 38:21 NKJV; Ps. 69:18a NRSV; Ps. 31:14 not paraphrased)

Prayers, Praises, and Personal Notes

_____

_____

_____

_____

Scripture Reading: John 20:24-29

Practicing the Spiritual Life

When the disciples told Thomas they'd seen Jesus, what was his response?

_____

_____

For what concerns are you struggling with unbelief?

_____

_____

Today look for and write down the ways you see Jesus' caring presence in your life.

_____

_____

Prayer

Jesus, You stood in the midst of Your disciples and said to them, "Peace be to you." But they were terrified and frightened, and supposed they had seen a spirit. And You said to them "Why are you troubled? And why do doubts arise in your hearts? Behold My hands and My feet, that it is I Myself; handle Me, and see; for a spirit has not flesh and bones, as you see I have." Though I have not seen You, Jesus, I love You; and even though I do not see You now, I believe in You and am filled with an inexpressible and glorious joy. (Luke 24:36-39 KJV; 1 Peter 1:8, all paraphrased)

Prayers, Praises, and Personal Notes

_____

_____

_____

Scripture Reading: Acts 12:5-17

Practicing the Spiritual Life

In Peter's shock, what did he think he was seeing as he was led out of prison, and what did he realize when it dawned on him that he'd been set free?

_____

_____

How did the Christians praying for Peter show their disbelief?

_____

_____

What answer to prayer has surprised you because you didn't expect it to come?

_____

_____

Prayer

O my Deliverer, "Turn your ear toward me. Rescue me quickly. Be a rock of refuge for me, a strong fortress to save me." "Pull me out of the mud; don't let me sink any deeper! Rescue me from those who hate me, and pull me from these deep waters." "O guard my life, and deliver me; do not let me be put to shame, for I take refuge in you." "Set me free from my prison, that I may praise your name. Then the righteous will gather about me because of your goodness to me." (Ps. 31:2 GOD'S WORD; Ps. 69:14 NLT; Ps. 25:20 NRSV; Ps. 142:7 not paraphrased)

Prayers, Praises, and Personal Notes

_____

_____

_____

Scripture Reading: Job 2:11-13

Practicing the Spiritual Life

How did Job's friends react when they saw him, and why were they so shocked?

_____

_____

_____

When you've been in shock, what was the most comfort to you, and why?

_____

_____

_____

Prayer

O Silent One, "the troubles of my heart have multiplied; free me from my anguish." "I said to myself, 'I will watch what I do and not sin in what I say.'" "But as I stood there in silence—not even speaking of good things—the turmoil within me grew to the bursting point." "I am silent before you; I won't say a word." Through Your tender mercy, O God, by which You, the Dayspring from on high, have visited me, give light to me as I sit in darkness and in the shadow of death, to guide my feet into the way of peace. Then my heart will sing to You and not be silent. O Lord my God, I will give You thanks forever. (Ps. 25:17; Ps. 39:1a-2, 9a NLT not paraphrased; Luke 1:78-79 NKJV; Ps. 30:12 paraphrased)

Prayers, Praises, and Personal Notes

_____

_____

_____

Scripture Reading: Job 3:1-3, 11-16

Practicing the Spiritual Life
In his state of shock what did Job curse? What did he long for?

_____

_____

In what ways can you relate to Job's request?

_____

_____

Describe a time when you experienced both shock and God-given peace.

_____

_____

Prayer
"O my God, I cry by day, but you do not answer; and by night, but find no rest." "If I say, 'Surely the darkness shall cover me, and the light around me become night,' even the darkness is not dark to you; the night is as bright as the day, for darkness is as light to you. For it was you who formed my inward parts; you knit me together in my mother's womb." "From birth I was cast upon you; from my mother's womb you have been my God." Therefore, "I will lie down in peace and sleep, for you alone, O Lord, will keep me safe." "Lord, you have brought light to my life; my God, you light up my darkness." (Ps. 22:2 NRSV; Ps. 139:11-13 NRSV; Ps. 22:10; Ps. 4:8 NLT; Ps. 18:28 NLT not paraphrased)

Prayers, Praises, and Personal Notes

_____

_____

_____

Scripture Reading: Job 3:11-23

Practicing the Spiritual Life

In his shock and disbelief what "why" questions did Job ask God?

_____

_____

What questions have you asked God regarding your trials?

_____

_____

This week search the Scriptures and ask the Lord for His answers to your questions. Then write down the answers He seems to give you.

_____

_____

Prayer

"Why, O Lord, do you reject me and hide your face from me?" "For You are the God of my strength; Why do You cast me off? Why do I go mourning because of the oppression of the enemy?" "Why, O Lord, do you stand far off? Why do you hide yourself in times of trouble?" "Even today my complaint is bitter; My hand is listless because of my groaning." "Turn and answer me, O Lord my God! Restore the light to my eyes." "For you are the fountain of life, the light by which we see." (Ps. 88:14; Ps. 43:2 NKJV; Ps. 10:1; Job 23:2 NKJV; Ps. 13:3a NLT; Ps. 36:9 NLT not paraphrased)

Prayers, Praises, and Personal Notes

_____

_____

_____

Scripture Reading: Job 3:24-26

Practicing the Spiritual Life
In what ways do you relate to Job's emotional reaction in his shock?

_____

_____

_____

Throughout the day take a few moments to rest in the Lord by giving your concerns to Him; write down how He helped you have a quiet heart.

_____

_____

_____

Prayer
"All my longings lie open before you, O Lord; my sighing is not hidden from you." "My tears have been my food day and night, while they continually say to me, 'Where is your God?'" "My life is consumed by anguish and my years by groaning; my strength fails because of my affliction, and my bones grow weak." O Lord, let Your lovingkindness be upon me, according as I have hoped in You. Grant me Your peace, the peace of Your kingdom at all times and in all ways under all circumstances and conditions, whatever comes. Lord be with me. (Ps. 38:9; Ps. 42:3 NKJV; Ps. 31:10 not paraphrased; Ps. 33:22 NAS95; 2 Thess. 3:16 AMP paraphrased)

Prayers, Praises, and Personal Notes

_____

_____

_____

WEEK THREE

Shattered by Sorrow

"My soul is weary with sorrow;
strengthen me according to your word."

PSALM 119:28

About thirty-five years ago, Ron and I were living in Portland, Oregon, when a hurricane-like storm struck. Now winds of that force were unheard of in the state, so we stood at our front bay window oblivious of the danger, watching debris flying everywhere. I shudder as I realize that we could have been seriously injured by shattered glass or even killed by our house collapsing.

We didn't recognize the severity of the storm until it passed and we drove through the streets. Portland looked as if an angry giant had stomped through the city, crushing one house or business and leaving others untouched or slightly damaged. The wind blew out windows, knocked down fireplace chimneys, and rolled cars and large mobile homes across highways as if they were tin toys. The storm ripped off huge branches from trees and felled power poles and lines. Streets and rivers were clogged with debris. Amazingly, our house was not damaged even though it sat on a knoll above the other houses on our street.

Shattered by Loss and Sorrow

Sorrow can strike us like a hurricane once shock and disbelief wear off. We wonder how we can survive such a crushing loss. We can suffer immense grief when storms of trials rip our lives apart, leaving behind shattered, broken hearts.

We can also lose our sense of personal identity and place, such as after the loss of a job or the death of a spouse. We don't know who we are without them. We feel as if part of us is missing and that we're not the persons we were before.

Gerald Sittser suffered the full force of a hurricane of sorrow after three of his family members were killed in a single accident. "That initial deluge of loss slowly gave way over the next months to the steady seepage of pain that comes when grief, like floodwaters refusing to subside, finds every crack and crevice of the human spirit to enter and erode. I thought that I was going to lose my mind."[1]

"The loss of anything of real value which a person cares about can produce grief. There seem to be important factors in understanding grief. Not only have I lost some*thing,* but it is something of value, something which has provided me with security or support or satisfaction and fulfillment, something in which I have been invested emotionally, something which I truly care about."[2]

The more we loved and cared about someone, the more of ourselves that we committed to a relationship or invested in our work or project, the more staggering our grief when we lose one of them.

Experiencing Grief

People express grief in different ways. They cry openly, need to weep alone, or show little or no emotion. They may collapse, become hysterical, or give others the impression that they're doing well.

When my friend Judie had cancer, women from her church drove her seventy miles for radiation treatments. She shared about her grief: "I remember lying on the sofa, crying as I waited for someone to pick me up. When it was time to leave, I'd dry my eyes, wash up, put a smile on my face, and go out that door. I tried not to burden the women with my grief."

Waves of sorrow, guilt, regrets, and remorse wash over us. "A wave of grief occurs when we become aware of the deep emptiness in ourselves resulting from a loss. . . . This mixture of feelings and physical reactions is called waves because, like waves along the seashore, they come with varied frequency and power."[3]

Mourning drains our energy, makes us more susceptible to illness, and increases our stress. We overeat or are unable to eat at all. We may be overcome by inner turmoil, emotional and mental conflicts, and irrational fears, especially of death. We feel as if we're drowning as we struggle to reach the surface and survive our grief.

Sorrow can cause such confusion that we don't know what we need to do or how to make rational decisions. We don't even realize that we're not functioning well. I thought I was handling my normal duties fine after Ron had heart surgery. Later when I prepared to have our taxes done, I discovered that during the time of his surgery and several months of recovery, our check register didn't make sense. I'd made all kinds of mistakes and written checks incorrectly, and our financial records were a mess.

Some people try to escape sorrow by working longer hours or keeping up a frenzied schedule. "It takes a lot of energy to cry or to feel rage, guilt, or frustration—sometimes all at once. Yet it takes even more energy to contain and defend against emotional outbursts when around others."[4]

Some stifle grief to remain strong for others and complete necessary tasks. Otherwise, they fear they will be so paralyzed by sorrow that they won't be able to function, meet the demands of life, and maintain a normal routine. If they ever let go and cry, they fear they'd lose control and "act crazy."

"Grief is so impossibly painful, so akin to panic, that ways must be invented to defend against the emotional onslaught of suffering. There is a fear that if one ever gives in fully to grief, one would be swept under—as in a huge tidal wave—never to surface to ordinary emotional stages again."[5]

My friend Judie recounted why she needed to contain her grief when she had Hodgkin's Disease:

"I was facing something so frightening, and I had to hold it together for my husband and daughters. But I was really holding it together for myself because I was so afraid. I couldn't even let myself know how upset I was. I couldn't let myself do what I wanted to do when I went for radiation treatments. I wanted to scream, 'You're not going to do this to me again!'

"I thought, *If I lose control, I'll never get it back. If I ever start crying, I'll never be able to stop.* The face I had to put on to make it easier on everybody else helped me hold myself together; it kept me from totally coming apart. I felt as if I were made of glass. If I ever broke, I wouldn't be able to put the pieces back together."

Grief Work

"Grief work is called grief work because that is precisely what it is—work. Grief needs to be worked through, worked out, worked off. And it *will be* somehow, somewhere, sometime—either constructively or destructively, partially or completely, in an integrating fashion or disintegrating, health restoring or health destroying, as good grief or bad grief, at the time of the loss or years removed."[6]

Morrie Schwartz, who had a fatal degenerative disease, wrote about how he worked through his grief:

"We ordinarily think of mourning for others—our parents and our other loved ones—but we don't think very much about mourning for ourselves. . . . I let myself experience the grief, the sadness, the despair, the bitterness, the anger, the dread, the regret, and the sense of finishing before my time. I let the tears flow until they dry up. . . . I'm crying about my own death, my departure from people I love, the sense of unfinished business. . . . Crying has helped me gradually come to accept the end. . . ."[7]

As we work through our own grief, we are more sensitive, vulnerable, and easily hurt by others. We need to realize that others will place unrealistic expectations upon us about how we should act or feel. They can be insensitive to the rawness of our pain. Some even tell us their heartbreaking stories and expect us to take care of them.

The ability to work through grief is different for each person. Some people grieve for months while others sorrow for a year or more after a loss or major change. The second year is often more painful than the first. After a loss or a series of severe trials, it can take two to five years to adjust to major changes, accept the losses, and feel released from deep sorrow.

The process is especially difficult when a heartache is ongoing and unresolved. Years later one may be struck by waves of grief, especially when dealing with complications related to that loss, such as a divorce. But we can experience the sadness of a loss and at the same time make a meaningful life for ourselves and those we love.

But we need to be careful that we don't become stuck in our sorrow. Years after a loss if we are still angry, bitter, depressed, and/or in deep mourning, then we haven't let go and moved on as we need to. We are locked into living in the past. Working with a Christian counselor can help us move beyond the past with its crippling emotions.

Past heartaches do not make new ones easier or less traumatic to go through. Past griefs may even intensify the sorrow of a present loss. Fresh grief can bring back sorrowful memories. Families and friends often gather and reminisce at a funeral not only about the loved one they've lost, but about others who have passed away as well. We need times to share losses in order to work through present heartaches.

Past griefs can also help us get through current losses. They make us more aware of how we must take care of ourselves, how to care for and comfort others, and how to deal with essential details and necessary rituals. Past losses can be a reminder of how the Lord cared for us during those times, how He comforted and supported us in sorrow. Realizing His faithfulness sustains us as we work through fresh grief.

Spiritual Sorrow

Emotional grief and spiritual sorrow are so alike that we may not realize the difference. In the spiritual reaction phase, this sorrow is the grief experienced when faith is tried and our trust in the Lord is tested during affliction and loss. We experience spiritual sorrow when we cannot comprehend why a loving God could permit such awful things to happen and/or go on for so long. We pray for relief, but the pain or problem grows worse. We question why God doesn't intervene, why He doesn't seem to answer when we call.

Christians, however, strongly disapprove of questioning God or expressing spiritual sorrow. They "view crying over loss as a lack of faith or trust, or lack of hope. They seem to maintain that religious faith and tears are incompatible; that a faith in God and belief in life after death make crying and grieving quite inappropriate. There is a subtle but strong suggestion that if grievers experience such feelings coming on, they would be wise to suppress them and thus witness to the strength of their faith."[8]

Scripture is filled with examples of godly people expressing spiritual sorrow. Can you relate to these? Job cried out, "Surely, O God, you have worn me out; you have devastated my entire household." "My face is red with weeping, deep shadows ring my eyes" (Job 16:7, 16).

Have you felt spiritually confused and off balance? "My confusion is continually before me, and the shame of my face hath covered me" (Ps. 44:15 KJV).

Do you wonder if God even hears? David cried, "'Hear my prayer, O Lord, listen to my cry for help; be not deaf to my weeping'" (Ps. 39:12).

Do you feel weak? David wept, "Be merciful to me, O Lord, for I am in distress; my eyes grow weak with sorrow, my soul and my body with grief" (Ps. 31:9).

Have you suffered anguish? "My life is consumed by anguish and my years by groaning; my strength fails because of my affliction, and my bones grow weak" (Ps. 31:10).

Have you been overcome by a broken heart? "How long must I wrestle with my thoughts and every day have sorrow in my heart?" (Ps. 13:2).

Do you think God is punishing you? "The arrows of the Almighty are in me, my spirit drinks in their poison; God's terrors are marshaled against me" (Job 6:4). Job didn't realize that it wasn't God harming him but Satan who had stirred up the wicked to attack him, and Satan does the same to us.

Finding Comfort in Spiritual Sorrow

If we are to maintain our faith, we need to realize that the Lord understands our questioning hearts and cares about our spiritual sorrow. Jesus, David, Esther, Jeremiah, Job, Naomi, and the apostle Paul, among others, suffered spiritual grief. These men and women demonstrate that it is possible to come through trials and emerge with stronger faith.

Jesus was acquainted with distresses, sicknesses, sorrows, and weaknesses, and He knows and cares about ours. When His friend Lazarus died, "Jesus wept" (John 11:35). Jesus was deeply moved with compassion and troubled in heart. Yes, Jesus wept, and those are two of the most comforting words in Scripture. If He mourned for His friend, does He not care about *our* tears?

"He was despised and rejected by men, a man of sorrows, and familiar with suffering." "Surely he took up our infirmities and carried our sorrows" (Isa. 53:3a, 4a). We have this assurance and comfort that the Lord has taken our pain upon Himself. We are loved, and He will guide and sustain us as we work through our spiritual grief.

The Lord is always available to hear our deepest expressions of grief and most anguished questions. He is our constant caregiver and our unfailing support. No matter how shattered we feel by our losses, we can find comfort in the faithfulness of the Lord.

GOD WAS FAITHFUL

I've had many heartaches in my life this year.
My heart has been broken, and I've shed many a tear.
My spirit was crushed, and it showed on my face,
but God revealed His love through His tender grace.
Though each sorrow seemed impossible to mend,
God was still faithful with His love to send.
With each of my losses God showed me His power.
He did this moment by moment and hour by hour.
God was faithful to me, and His love was outpoured,
So each step of the way I'm trusting the Lord.[9]

Scripture Reading: 1 Samuel 20:1-4, 12-17, 41-42

Practicing the Spiritual Life

How did David and Jonathan comfort each other in their grief, and what was their spiritual commitment to each other?

_____

_____

_____

With what friend/s can you pray and share your griefs? If you need Christian friends for mutual support, ask the Lord to lead you to them.

_____

_____

_____

Prayer

Even now, Lord, You are my witness in heaven, my Advocate on high, my Intercessor, and my Friend, as my eyes pour out tears to You. On my behalf plead with God as You plead for Your friends. Rescue me from my powerful enemy, from my foes, who are too strong for me. Hear my voice, O God, in my meditation; preserve my life from fear of the enemy. (Job 16:19-21; 2 Sam. 22:18; Ps. 64:1 NKJV, all paraphrased)

Prayers, Praises, and Personal Notes

_____

_____

_____

_____

_____

_____

Scripture Reading: Psalm 13

Practicing the Spiritual Life

In his grief what questions did David ask God?

_____

_____

How did David affirm his trust in the Lord?

_____

_____

Write your own questions to the Lord and then statements affirming your trust in Him.

_____

_____

Prayer

Arise, Lord! Lift up your hand. Do not forget me, for I am helpless. "O Lord, how long will this go on? Will you hide yourself forever?" "How long must I wait? When will you punish those who persecute me?" "I am sick at heart. How long, O Lord, until you restore me?" "I weep with grief; encourage me by your word." "I am in trouble, so do not hide your face from me. Answer me quickly!" I truly trust in You, Lord. Because You, O God Most High, always love me, I will not be overwhelmed. (Ps. 10:12 paraphrased; Ps. 89:46a NLT; Ps. 119:84 NLT; Ps. 6:3 NLT; Ps. 119:28 NLT; Ps. 69:17 GOD'S WORD not paraphrased; Ps. 21:7 NCV paraphrased)

Prayers, Praises, and Personal Notes

_____

_____

_____

Scripture Reading: Psalm 39:12-13

Practicing the Spiritual Life

What did David ask the Lord to do?

_____

_____

About what have you cried out to God for a hearing and asked Him not to
be deaf to your requests?

_____

_____

During what trying situations has the Lord heard the cries of your heart?

_____

_____

Prayer

"Listen to my cry for help, O God. Pay attention to my prayer." "My eyes
fail from weeping, I am in torment within." "Have pity on me! O Lord, be
my helper!" "O God, do not remain silent. Do not turn a deaf ear to me. Do
not keep quiet, O God." "O Lord, listen to my prayer. Open your ears to hear
my urgent requests. Answer me because you are faithful and righteous." "I
call on you, O God, for you will answer me; give ear to me and hear my
prayer." (Ps. 61:1 GOD'S WORD; Lam. 2:11a; Ps. 30:10b GOD'S WORD; Ps.
83:1 GOD'S WORD; Ps. 143:1 GOD'S WORD; Ps. 17:6 not paraphrased)

Prayers, Praises, and Personal Notes

_____

_____

_____

Scripture Reading: Job 6:1-3

Practicing the Spiritual Life
How did Job feel in his grief?

_____

_____

In what heartaches have you felt weighed down by grief?

_____

_____

In what ways has the Lord encouraged and lifted you up in sorrow?

_____

_____

Prayer
"My soul is in anguish. How long, O Lord, how long?" Why do You hide Your face from me and forget my misery and oppression? You have walled me in so that I cannot escape; You have weighed me down with chains. "Turn, O Lord, and deliver me; save me because of your unfailing love." "I will exalt you, O Lord, for you lifted me out of the depths." (Ps. 6:3 not paraphrased; Ps. 44:24; Lam. 3:7 paraphrased; Ps. 6:4; Ps. 30:1a not paraphrased)

Prayers, Praises, and Personal Notes

_____

_____

_____

_____

_____

Scripture Reading: Job 6:4

Practicing the Spiritual Life
What did Job think God was doing to him?

_____

_____

In your spiritual grief, have you ever thought that God had set Himself against you? If so, in what ways?

_____

_____

Today how is the Lord displaying His unfailing love for you?

_____

_____

Prayer
Almighty God, You have heaped disasters upon me and shot me down with Your arrows. "Your fierce anger has overwhelmed me. Your terrors have cut me off." "For calamity from God is a terror to me, and because of His majesty I can do nothing." "Reach down your hand from on high; deliver me and rescue me." "Let the morning bring me word of your unfailing love, for I have put my trust in you. Show me the way I should go, for to you I lift up my soul." (Deut. 32:23 NLT paraphrased; Ps. 88:16 NLT; Job 31:23 NAS95; Ps. 144:7a; Ps. 143:8 not paraphrased)

Prayers, Praises, and Personal Notes

_____

_____

_____

Scripture Reading: Job 6:6-7

Practicing the Spiritual Life

How did Job feel about food when he was grief stricken?

_____

_____

When you're sad, do you eat for comfort, or are you unable to eat?

_____

_____

Find and meditate on one of the prayers today that can give you spiritual nourishment and comfort.

_____

_____

Prayer

"My heart is beaten down and withered like grass because I have forgotten about eating." "I eat ashes like bread and my tears are mixed with my drink." All my days I eat in darkness, and I have much sorrow and sickness and anger. O satisfy me early with Your mercy and unfailing love that I may rejoice and be glad all my days. Then "my soul will be satisfied as with the richest of foods; with singing lips my mouth will praise you." (Ps. 102:4, 9 GOD'S WORD not paraphrased; Eccl. 5:17 NKJV; Ps. 90:14 KJV paraphrased; Ps. 63:5 not paraphrased)

Prayers, Praises, and Personal Notes

_____

_____

_____

Scripture Reading: Job 6:8-13

Practicing the Spiritual Life

In his despair and spiritual grief, what did Job say he wanted God to do?

_____

_____

Have you ever been in spiritual grief? If so, what did you want the Lord to do for you?

_____

_____

For what sorrow do you need the Lord to strengthen your heart and renew your hope?

_____

_____

Prayer

Grant me the desire of my heart and do not withhold the request of my lips. "Lord, don't be far away. You are my strength; hurry to help me." My bones are dried up and my hope has perished. I am completely cut off. I wait in hope for You, Lord; You are my help and my shield. I'll be patient and wait on You; I'll be of good courage. O strengthen my heart, and I will wait patiently on You, Lord. (Ps. 21:2 paraphrased; Ps. 22:19 NCV not paraphrased; Ezek. 37:11b NAS95; Ps. 33:20; Ps. 27:14 KJV paraphrased)

Prayers, Praises, and Personal Notes

_____

_____

_____

Secondary Losses

"The truth is, a kernel of wheat must be planted in the soil.
Unless it dies it will be alone—a single seed.
But its death will produce many new kernels—
a plentiful harvest of new lives.
Those who love their life in this world will lose it.
Those who despise their life in this world
will keep it for eternal life."

JOHN 12:24-25 NLT

About fifteen years ago during a torrential rainstorm in California, the mobile home park where my parents lived was flooded so quickly they had to be evacuated. My father had started to prepare lunch, and when I picked them up at the flood shelter, the only belongings he'd managed to rescue were a whole uncooked chicken and a few clothes. Later we teased him about the rescued chicken, but dealing with the aftermath of the flood was not so humorous. My parents lost many of their possessions. They were displaced from their home for months while contractors replaced the floor and repaired water-damaged walls.

Primary and Secondary Losses

A primary loss such as a death, divorce, serious illness, or natural disaster includes many secondary losses and complications. My parents had many losses due to the flood, including appliances, carpet, drapes, and furniture. The most difficult losses were keepsakes and photographs.

Secondary losses can also be emotional, physical, psychological, and spiritual; we feel and experience them. They include depression; emotional and physical distress; loss of bodily functions, identity, self-esteem, and productivity; loss of status after being laid off from a job or retired; loss of appetite, energy, and restful sleep; loss of faith and commitment to serving the Lord.

Secondary losses include the many adjustments and changes we have to make in our lives. Such losses consume our energy and time because of added responsibilities or the need to take care of others.

People experience emotional losses when they feel their lives have lost all meaning. Their emotions seesaw between wanting to live and wishing to die, being grateful for life and despising it, wanting God to be with them and to leave them alone. Job cried to God, "I despise my life; I would not live forever. Let me alone; my days have no meaning" (Job 7:16).

We feel as if our days and nights are dragging on endlessly or that time is moving too swiftly without any hope in sight. Moreover, we can lose all sense of time. We cannot remember what day it is; one day moves into the next in a blur. We barely recall events that happened the day or a week before a loss. After a series of severe trials, I've often felt as if twenty years have passed instead of only a few months.

After a major loss, some people have accidents or frequent or serious illnesses. If they're in the hospital, they feel lost without the familiar comforts of home. When they're sick and dependent upon others for care, they feel as if they've lost their independence and personal dignity.[1]

My friend Judie told about the secondary losses she experienced before and after her extensive cancer surgery: "I was at a teaching hospital and was often examined by five or six doctors at a time. I felt that they did not look at me as a person but as a cancer specimen under a magnifying glass. My body was barely covered while doctors examined me and talked to each other as if I weren't there. I felt humiliated and wanted to hide.

"My body was never the same after surgery and radiation. I am a twenty-year survivor of cancer, but emotionally and physically the scars will be with me for a lifetime."

Change as a Secondary Loss

Feelings of loss can be caused by major or minor life changes. "Change in itself always involves a loss. At the very least, it is a loss of the status quo, of the way things were. This is why, whether a change is positive or negative, there is always some dimension of loss to it, with some measure of grief being warranted even if it is negligible."[2]

When adversity strikes, life as we knew it can come to a screeching halt. We are forced to make a sudden detour. We have to change plans, schedules, and basic pattern of living. We not only have to maintain normal duties but also carry extra responsibilities. We lose the rhythm of routine that provides us with a sense of security.

After devastating losses, people's lives change so much they feel as if they've been traveling great distances. They have journeyed so far away from life the way it was before that they are confused and lost. They cannot go back, and they aren't sure what direction they're going. Moreover, they can't see any resemblance between the persons they are today and the way they were in the past.

One of the secondary losses we suffer has to do with our expectations about the future. "We are also dealing with the loss of those purposes that determined not only how our life had been but also how we thought our life would be in the future."[3] If our child or a loved one dies, we grieve about the future he or she might have had. Sorrow can resurface on his or her birthday, the anniversary of the person's death, or at special occasions he or she has missed.

Bearing the Impact of Losses

Some losses slightly impact us, while others permanently change the course of our lives. The degree of impact and grief will depend upon how much we care. Losing a job we don't like and are not financially dependent on won't hurt as much as losing our sole means of support.

Bearing the impact of things we've missed out on in life can be painful. We may have wanted to do a certain kind of work but were unable to achieve it. A single friend of mine expressed grief over not being married, having children, or owning a home.

The impact of a painful childhood can cause grief. Naomi's parents were violent alcoholics, and she told about her feelings of loss: "I was overwhelmed by the hurts of my childhood. I felt I lost so many of my adult years trying to grow up, heal, and overcome fears and deep insecurities. I wonder what kind of person I might have been if I'd been raised in a loving Christian home."

One of the most painful impacts of loss can come as a result of sin, particularly of a destructive habit or pattern of behavior. Most of us have to live with the regrets and consequences of hurtful choices that have wounded others, whether intentional or unintentional.

The Lord forgives us as we confess our sins and repent, which includes changing our attitude and behavior. The heartache comes when we desire to restore relationships but can't. Even when we take responsibility for our wrongdoing, we still have to live with painful consequences.

Loss of Emotional and Spiritual Comfort

An especially painful secondary loss comes when close friends and family whom we were sure we could count on abandon us and do not give us the support we need. This can also occur when families disagree about what to do and how to handle a difficult trial. People avoid talking to us about a loss or death, which can be a death in itself.

Some Christians are judgmental and presume to speak on God's behalf while advising others how they should respond to heartaches. When Christians proudly profess "super faith," they make those who are hurting feel spiritually inferior. Reprimanding others for their lack of trust in the Lord is also hurtful.

Eliphaz, the first friend who replied to Job's anguished cries, used the name of God to strike his most hurtful blows. "All these circumstances must be proof enough to you," said this friend, "that I do not censure you myself; that it is by the Spirit of God that I do it, and that God, who manifests and communicates Himself to me, has shown me your error and your pride."[4]

Eliphaz exhorted Job, "My advice to you is this: Go to God and present your case to him. For he does great works too marvelous to understand. He performs miracles without number" (Job 5:8-9 NLT).

What Eliphaz said about God is true, but saying it to Job with a judgmental attitude was hurtful. The totality of Job's losses and his raw sorrow were ignored by Eliphaz. This "friend" had the audacity to promise Job health while he was desperately ill, wealth when he'd lost everything, and many more descendants when his children, who were crushed to death, lay fresh in their graves (Job 4-5).

One commentator points out that Job asserts "over and over that, to his knowledge, he is not guilty of any particular sin terrible enough to have caused him the suffering he is experiencing. But while he asserts and declares his innocence of a particular known sin, Job does not deny his sinful state and nature. Several times he refers to the fact that he is a sinner, guilty of sins that no soap can wash away (7:21; 9:28, 29; 14:4)."[5]

Job's friends were judgmental counselors, speaking for God and making promises on His behalf, saying what can only be said by God Himself. In the end the Lord reprimanded those friends for judging Job wrongly.

Oswald Chambers wrote about a woman whose husband and child were murdered while they were serving as missionaries. She told Chambers about the "blank amazed agony of those days—'We did not feel, we did not pray, we were dazed with sorrow.' She was shown a lock of her little child's golden hair and was told that both husband and child had been discovered murdered, beheaded and naked."

After this missionary wife returned home to England, she said that she did not "doubt God, but—'He did not answer prayer.' 'Oh, how many prayed for my husband, good valued servant of God, all to no avail.' In those days of dull dreary reaction the people who nearly drove her wild with distress were those who knew chapter and verse, the 'why' and 'wherefore' of her suffering and grief."

While those people chattered away, she cried in her heart, "How long, O Lord, how long?" One day while she was lying on the sofa, a minister friend of her husband's came quietly into the room, kissed her forehead, and left without saying a word. She began to heal from that point on.[6]

Suffering Loss for Spiritual Gain

During the spiritual reaction phase, secondary losses and complications can cause us to doubt the Lord. We may question: What does the Lord desire to accomplish in our lives through trials? How can affliction possibly be used to our spiritual benefit?

In the following passage we discover the principle of suffering loss for spiritual gain. "Then he (Jesus) called his disciples and the crowds to come over and listen. 'If any of you wants to be my follower,' he told them, 'you must put aside your selfish ambition, shoulder your cross, and follow me. If you try to keep your life for yourself, you will lose it. But if you give up your life for my sake and for the sake of the Good News, you will find true life. And how do you benefit if you gain the whole world but lose your own soul in the process? Is anything worth more than your soul?'" (Mark 8:34-37 NLT).

First, the loss we must suffer for spiritual gain is the willingness to come after Christ and deny ourselves for His sake. "Jesus Christ asks us to give up the best we have got to Him, our right to our self. Self-realization must be renounced in order that Jesus Christ may realize Himself in us."[7]

Commentator Matthew Henry pointed out that Christ calls us to deny our desires for constant gratification and cravings for things—for His sake, for the good of others, even our enemies. We're to deny our sense of self-importance for the sake of our own personal and spiritual well-being.[8] "For the world offers only the lust for physical pleasure, the lust for everything we see, and pride in our possessions. These are not from the Father. They are from this evil world" (1 John 2:16 NLT).

The second loss we must suffer for spiritual gain is the willingness to daily take up our own cross. The cross we must carry includes "providential afflictions, persecutions for righteousness' sake, every trouble that befalls us."[9] Few of us are willing to live the crucified life, at least until afflictions force us to. Are we willing to carry our cross so we can gain a more intimate relationship with Christ and glorify Him? Or are we carrying our cross with bitterness, a rebellious heart, because we have no other choice? If we rebel at the cross, we have not truly abandoned ourselves to the Lord.

"There is a possibility that you might make a mistake concerning your abandonment to the Lord. You may abandon yourself to the Lord hoping and expecting always to be caressed and loved and spiritually blessed by Him. . . . If you gave yourself to Him to be *blessed* and to be *loved,* you cannot suddenly turn around and take back your life at another season . . . when you are being *crucified!*"[10]

"I have been crucified with Christ; it is no longer I who live, but Christ lives in me; and the life which I now live in the flesh I live by faith in the Son of God, who loved me and gave Himself for me" (Gal. 2:20 NKJV). True abandonment is sharing in Christ's crucifixion. It means giving up all claim to ourselves, all control of our lives, and surrendering ourselves entirely to Him by faith.

"Sometimes you may bear the cross in weakness; at other times you may bear the cross in strength, but whether you bear it in weakness or in strength, *bear it!* Both weakness and strength should be the same to us since we bear the cross in the will of God."[11]

More often I bear the cross in weakness. My trust gives way; I feel sorry for myself. I fall apart emotionally. How can I live a self-sacrificing life for Christ when it requires all the energy I have to survive my pain and take care of myself and those I love?

Today as I write, I am awaiting ten weeks of treatments for a painful bladder condition that has plagued me for more than forty years. My husband, Ron, is awaiting laser eye surgery to repair hemorrhaging blood vessels caused by his diabetes.

How can the Lord expect me to do His will in the midst of suffering? How can I accomplish anything at all for Him when the burning pain is so intense I can barely concentrate? I can't accomplish His will on my own, but I must. I am totally accountable and responsible to be the person Christ wants me to be and to be obedient to what He's called me to do. Yet I feel entirely incapable and unqualified.

Forty-three years ago the Lord gave me Philippians 4:13 as my life verse. "I can do all things through Christ who strengthens me" (NKJV). No other verse could have been more prophetic and true of my life. Over and over again

I've had to learn in my many weaknesses that I can accomplish the Lord's will by His strength.

Third, the loss we must suffer for spiritual gain is to follow Christ wherever He takes us. Once we voluntarily come after Him, He will guide us on the journey He has planned for us. But that road may not be easy. He may lead us through fires and floods of afflictions.

Fourth, the loss we must suffer for spiritual gain is to lose our life for Christ's sake and for the Gospel's. "'Present your bodies a living sacrifice'—go to the funeral of your own independence. It is not a question of giving up sin, but of giving up my right to myself, my natural independence and self-assertiveness."[12]

When we begin to understand what it means to give up the right to ourselves, we may cry, "Impossible!" Why? Because losing ourselves for Christ means dying to self. We fear the death of our independence. Yet this death process is the only way we can produce new spiritual life. "I tell you the truth, unless a grain of wheat falls to the ground and dies, it remains only a single seed. But if it dies, it produces many seeds" (John 12:24).

Fifth, the loss we must suffer for spiritual gain is to voluntarily give up the world to gain life in Christ. "One soul is worth more than all the world; our own souls are of greater value to us than all the wealth, honor, and pleasures of this present time, if we had them." Gaining "the world is often the losing of the soul."[13]

When we think of giving up the whole world, that seems so huge, so impossible. But it's the trivial worldly things that keep us from gaining Christ. It's the poor use of time, a negative attitude, a habit we won't give up. The willingness to give up daily many small things for Christ makes up the whole of commitment.

"Therefore I tell you, do not worry about your life, what you will eat or drink; or about your body, what you will wear. Is not life more important than food, and the body more important than clothes?" (Matt. 6:25).

"We argue in exactly the opposite way, even the most spiritual of us—'I *must* live, I *must* make so much money, I *must* be clothed and fed.' That is how it begins; the great concern of the life is not God but how we are going to fit ourselves to live. Jesus Christ says, 'Reverse the order, get rightly related to Me first, see that you maintain that as the great care of your life, and never put the concentration of your care on the other things.'"[14]

Living for Spiritual Gain

The apostle Paul showed us how to live out the principle of suffering loss for spiritual gain. The cost of that gain, however, was that Paul suffered extraordinary afflictions. "Second Corinthians 6, verses 4-10, are Paul's spiritual diary; they describe the outward hardships which proved the hot-bed for the graces of the Spirit—the working together of outward hardships and inward grace."[15]

Paul suffered a relentless series of crushing trials. "In everything we do, we try to show that we are true ministers of God. We patiently endure troubles and hardships and calamities of every kind. We have been beaten, been put in jail, faced angry mobs, worked to exhaustion, endured sleepless nights, and gone without food." "We have been beaten within an inch of our lives" (2 Cor. 6:4-5, 9b NLT).

Paul demonstrated faithfulness in affliction. "We have proved ourselves by our purity, our understanding, our patience, our kindness, our sincere love, and the power of the Holy Spirit. We have faithfully preached the truth. God's power has been working in us" (2 Cor. 6:6-7a NLT).

Paul's character and reputation were attacked. But for the sake of following Christ, Paul accepted the good with evil, loss for gain. The losses Paul endured for spiritual gain included being dishonored; regarded as a deceiver, liar, and impostor; experiencing sorrow, poverty, lack of recognition, slander, and false accusations.

Other Christians upheld Paul's character and honored him for his ministry. Paul's gains included honor, glory, recognition, a good reputation for being genuine and true, and "possessing all things in Christ"; the ability to rejoice always; and an effective ministry of making many people rich in faith.

If we're going to have an enduring faith and serve the Lord wholeheartedly, we need to realize that blessings are mixed with burdens, happiness with heartaches. Though our losses make us poor, we can become rich in spiritual gain.

"In all these things, display in your life a drawing on the grace of God, which will show evidence to yourself and to others that you are a miracle of His. Draw on His grace now, not later. The primary word in the spiritual vocabulary is *now*. Let circumstances take you where they will, but keep drawing on the grace of God in whatever condition you may find yourself."[16]

Scripture Reading: Mark 8:34

Practicing the Spiritual Life

What does Christ call us to do, and what loss must we suffer for spiritual gain?

_____

_____

_____

In which areas of your life do you need to deny yourself, take up your cross, and follow Christ?

_____

_____

_____

Prayer

Jesus, I want to be Your disciple; I must come and follow You, because as Your servant I must be where You are. And if I follow You, the Father will honor me. I must deny myself, for if I do not carry my cross and follow You, I cannot be Your disciple. But I have been crucified with You, Christ, and I no longer live, but You live in me. The life I live in the body, I live by faith in You, Son of God, who loves me and gave Yourself for me. (John 12:26 NLT; Luke 14:27; Gal. 2:20, all paraphrased)

Prayers, Praises, and Personal Notes

_____

_____

_____

_____

_____

Scripture Reading: Mark 8:35

Practicing the Spiritual Life

For whom are we to lose our lives?

_____

_____

_____

In what specific ways would Jesus have you lose your life for His sake and the Gospel's?

_____

_____

_____

Prayer

O my Security, if I try to make my life secure, I will lose it, but if I lose my life, I will keep it. "The truth is, a kernel of wheat must be planted in the soil. Unless it dies it will be alone—a single seed. But its death will produce many new kernels—a plentiful harvest of new lives." And if I love my life in this world, I will lose it. If I despise my life in this world, I will keep it for eternity. (Luke 17:33 NRSV paraphrased; John 12:24 NLT not paraphrased; John 12:25 NLT paraphrased)

Prayers, Praises, and Personal Notes

_____

_____

_____

_____

_____

Scripture Reading: Mark 8:36-37

Practicing the Spiritual Life

If we live only to gain the world, what do we lose?

_____

_____

What do you crave, lust for, and find pride in that you need to give up?

_____

_____

Today commit yourself to giving up one thing for the sake of gaining life in Christ.

_____

_____

Prayer

O Lord of my Life, the world offers me only the lust for physical pleasure, the lust for everything I see, and pride in my possessions. These are not from You, Father. They are from this evil world. And this world is fading away, along with everything I crave. Therefore, Jesus, as You've said to do, I won't worry about everyday life—whether I have enough food, drink, and clothes. Life consists of more than food and clothing. I look at the birds. They don't need to plant or harvest or put food in barns because, heavenly Father, You feed them. And I am far more valuable to You than they are. (1 John 2:16-17a NLT; Matt. 6:25-26 NLT, all paraphrased)

Prayers, Praises, and Personal Notes

_____

_____

_____

Scripture Reading: 2 Corinthians 6:4-10

Practicing the Spiritual Life

What severe hardships did Paul suffer for spiritual gain and to glorify Christ?

_____

_____

_____

What godly attributes would you like to demonstrate in suffering?

_____

_____

_____

Prayer

Ever-caring Comforter, "The suffering you sent was good for me, for it taught me to pay attention to your principles." So "do not be far from me, for trouble is near and there is no one to help." Oh, that I may persevere and endure hardships for Your name and not grow weary. Strengthen me with all power according to Your glorious might so that I may have great endurance and patience. Now let this encourage me to endure persecution patiently and remain firm to the end, obeying Your commands and trusting in You, Jesus. (Ps. 119:71 NLT; Ps. 22:11 not paraphrased; Rev. 2:3; Col. 1:11; Rev. 14:12 NLT paraphrased)

Prayers, Praises, and Personal Notes

_____

_____

_____

_____

_____

Scripture Reading: 2 Corinthians 6:4-10

Practicing the Spiritual Life

How did Paul respond to the hardships and attacks upon his character and reputation?

_____

_____

_____

How would the Lord have you respond in your trials?

_____

_____

_____

Prayer

Lord and Savior, "I know very well how foolish the message of the cross sounds to those who are on the road to destruction. But we who are being saved recognize this message as the very power of God." So I must never be ashamed to tell others about You, Lord. And I won't be ashamed of Christians either, even those in prison for You, Christ. With the strength You give me, I'll be ready to suffer with them for the proclamation of the Good News. So, as one who has been chosen by You, as one holy and beloved, I will put on a heart of compassion, kindness, humility, gentleness, and patience. I will set an example for the believers in speech, in life, in love, in faith, and in purity. (1 Cor. 1:18 NLT not paraphrased; 2 Tim. 1:8 NLT; Col. 3:12 NAS95; 1 Tim. 4:12b paraphrased)

Prayers, Praises, and Personal Notes

_____

_____

_____

Scripture Reading: Job 7:1-7

Practicing the Spiritual Life

What did Job say about the days and nights as he struggled with his feelings of loss?

_____

_____

In what ways do you relate to Job's major loss followed by so many other secondary losses and complications?

_____

_____

Look for and write down some of the simple provisions that help you find hope in the Lord.

_____

_____

Prayer

Merciful Lord, "Night pierces my bones; my gnawing pains never rest." "My life is no longer than the width of my hand. An entire lifetime is just a moment to you; human existence is but a breath." Now "I have only a little time left, so leave me alone—that I may have a little moment of comfort." "Though you have made me see troubles, many and bitter . . . restore my life again; from the depths of the earth you will again bring me up." "You shall increase my greatness, and comfort me on every side." (Job 30:17; Ps. 39:5 NLT; Job 10:20 NLT; Ps. 71:20; Ps. 71:21 NKJV not paraphrased)

Prayers, Praises, and Personal Notes

_____

_____

_____

Scripture Reading: Job 12:2-4; 13:1-2; 16:1-5

Practicing the Spiritual Life

What did Job say to defend himself against his friends' accusations?

_____

_____

During what heartaches have you felt judged and spiritually inferior to others?

_____

_____

How have others comforted and encouraged you in tough times?

_____

_____

Prayer

O my Deliverer, "I have become the ridicule of all my people—their taunting song all the day." "God has made my name a curse word; people spit in my face. My sight has grown weak because of my sadness, and my body is as thin as a shadow." "I am poor and helpless; God, hurry to me. You help me and save me. Lord, do not wait." Surely You will listen to my cry and comfort me. Now, Lord Jesus Christ and God my Father, who loved me and by Your grace gave me eternal encouragement and good hope, encourage my heart and strengthen me. (Lam. 3:14 NKJV; Job 17:6-7 NCV; Ps. 70:5 NCV not paraphrased; Ps. 10:17b NLT; 2 Thess. 2:16-17a paraphrased)

Prayers, Praises, and Personal Notes

_____

_____

_____

Dealing with Denial

*"Dear friends, do not be surprised
at the painful trial you are suffering,
as though something strange were happening to you.
But rejoice that you participate in the sufferings of Christ,
so that you may be overjoyed when his glory is revealed."*

1 PETER 4:12-13

*M*y friend Judie tells about her first reaction to the frightening news that she had cancer:

"When I went to my physician to have a lump on my neck checked, he told me it might be cancer. But it blew right over the top of my head, and I went into denial. He sent me to a specialist who did a biopsy. When the results came back, the doctor called my husband, Ted, at work and told him that it was cancer. Ted told me when he picked me up at my workplace, and I said, 'No, it can't be.'

"When we got home, our girls were in the bedroom laughing. I remember thinking, *Will I ever see my girls grow up?* My daughters were only five, nine, and twelve at the time.

"I went to the Stanford medical center for a second opinion. The first doctor who saw me said I had Hodgkin's disease. The only person I'd heard about with that kind of cancer had died. *I have three girls to raise. No, it can't be,* I kept thinking. *This is a bad dream, and it isn't going to happen.*

"A series of tests confirmed that it was Hodgkin's. Two weeks later I went back to Stanford for exploratory surgery. I had to wait until I was well enough for radiation treatments. During that month reality began to sink in as the tumors in my neck grew rapidly.

"Radiation treatments were especially difficult. Sometimes I felt that it wasn't really me going through this. On one level I knew it was real, but on another level I couldn't believe it. I had this feeling—I'm here, but I'm not really here.

"When my cancer was cured, I was in denial that it could come back. For years afterward just going for a checkup made me realize that it could return. Those were extremely frightening trips.

"Even now twenty years later, it seems that someone else had cancer. Part of me is still in denial. I would like to believe that it never really happened to me even though it did."

Denial

"Denial is a psychological buffer that protects us from knowledge or feelings we're not yet ready to deal with mentally, emotionally, or spiritually. All of us deny reality we're not ready to accept."[1]

Denial allows us a brief reprieve from facing a loss. It is a survival reaction and a means of self-protection that we use as a defense against painful reality. We go into denial when we're frightened and overwhelmed by a loss or when we don't know what to do or how to handle a trying situation. When we're in denial, we use whatever defenses necessary to keep ourselves from facing the truth.

Some people move in and out of denial. "Yes, it's serious." "No, it's nothing to worry about." Others overemphasize the positive and minimize serious complications. They contradict themselves, speaking openly about their painful experiences one moment, and then shift into denial, talking and acting as if everything is going to be fine.

Still others are not able to face the long-term implications of a loss and/or that their lives will never be the same. They try to believe that everything will return to normal.

A natural reaction to painful reality, denial gets us through the initial shock and helps us collect ourselves so we can deal with our loss. Realizing that we're in denial, letting go of it, and facing reality is a gradual but necessary part of the healing process.

Unhealthy Denial

Unhealthy denial is the persistent inability to acknowledge a loss or admit the truth about a painful situation. We're in unhealthy denial when we keep our distance from loved ones even when the problem is critical and requires our involvement. We avoid those who are suffering because we can't face the heartache or deal with their pain. But when we avoid others, their feelings of abandonment are intensified.

One of the most hurtful forms of denial is making false promises of God's blessings to people who have suffered a painful loss. Eliphaz said to Job, "He shall deliver you in six troubles. Yes, in seven no evil shall touch you" (Job 5:19 NKJV). Then Eliphaz listed all that God would do for Job. This was a cruel consolation and a denial of Job's grief, considering the loss of his health, ten children, servants, and the destruction and theft of all that he owned.

Denial is unhealthy when all the signs and symptoms of a serious problem exist, but we keep minimizing the severity of them. Problems avoided don't get better on their own. They become worse, and we are often unprepared and shocked by the devastating repercussions. Denial prevents openness and truthfulness. People cannot work together to deal with painful problems in a godly and healthy way.

Some people deny their own or a loved one's addiction, abuse, neglect, irresponsibility, mental illness, or dependence upon alcohol or another chemical. This denial can cause a lifetime of harm and hurt. It can cost a great deal—loss of a job, health, essential relationships, home, and belongings.

Some people determine how others should cope with a trial and in effect deny the sufferers' feelings. These people demand "appropriate" responses and urge others to repress their anger, fear, and grief.

We lose touch with reality when we deny the truth about a loss or wrongful situation, minimize the seriousness of it, and disassociate ourselves. The unwillingness to face trials intensifies the pain for ourselves and others.

We can reach the point of such extreme denial that we believe in and live a lie. We refuse to listen to others when they speak about a problem or loss. We resist and hinder other people's efforts to face and cope with a trying situation. Our denial confuses others and causes them to question their own perception of reality. Denial doesn't make sense, and it can be "crazy-making" for people who are doing what is necessary to handle a painful loss or problem.

Moreover, denial is unhealthy when we do not take responsibility for our contribution to a problem but blame others. We may, on the other hand, take all the blame without holding others accountable.

Facing Reality

Facing reality means that we accept the truth, realize the seriousness of a loss or problem, and take care of our responsibilities. Admitting our powerlessness to overcome problems alone and our need for help and prayer is a necessary step toward dealing with painful trials. If we need to protect ourselves or others from abusive and harmful situations, it's critical to seek help from a Christian counselor and/or pastor.

We are better able to face reality when we can talk about a loss or trial in an honest, open way with a trusted Christian friend. This helps us gain insights into the problem and discover what we need to do. We can be assured that the Lord will guide and support us as we work through this healing process.

The most difficult part of dealing realistically with heartaches is the realization that there is nothing more one can do. Those who have had a debilitating disease know the discouragement of following the doctor's instructions and taking necessary medicine only to have the condition worsen. Or someone does her best to heal a broken relationship, but it cannot be restored. Or the other person is unable to face reality. Or people go through counseling, deal openly with a serious problem, and pray their hearts out—but nothing changes.

Facing reality does not necessarily mean we can solve the problem or change painful situations. Being realistic will help us work through our grief, but remaining stuck in denial prevents us from getting through the healing process.

Spiritual Denial

During the spiritual reaction phase, denial is a protection we use against an unbelievable loss that we know the Lord has allowed. Spiritual denial is continuing to believe God will intervene even though we've experienced an irreversible loss. This denial is a normal response to a loss as long as it is only a temporary defense against the painful truth.

There is a fine line between spiritual denial and believing faith. God still works in miraculous ways. Broken families are reunited. People who were adamant unbelievers come to know Christ as Savior. Alcoholics and chemically dependent people are freed from their addictions. Loved ones near death recover and live.

John, a church custodian, was a prayer warrior. He interceded for many people early every morning in the church sanctuary. He also had a prison ministry. When he was diagnosed with terminal cancer, the doctors said John only had a short time to live. The prisoners as well as his church family fervently prayed for his healing. When John went to see the doctor many months later, he was astounded that John was still alive. God healed him, and he lived to serve the Lord many more years before he passed away.

How many times, however, have we prayed with the same faith, and the Lord's answer was no. God's ways and sovereign choices are a mystery.

What is the difference between spiritual denial and faith? We believe by faith that God can do the impossible; at the same time we face the painful truth. We seek the Lord's guidance so we can do whatever is necessary to solve a problem and/or deal with a loss. When there is nothing we can do, we continue to pray, asking the Lord for His will to be done.

When we are in spiritual denial, we *presume* that God will do the impossible. We put our faith in the "answer," not in God. Our minds are set on what we desire and closed to what He may allow. When the waiting goes on too long or God doesn't answer the way we expected, we may continue demanding that He do what we want. As a result, we become disappointed and even angry with God. We also blame ourselves or others for lack of faith, spiritual weakness, or negative thoughts that hindered the desired answer.

When we're in spiritual denial, we put the entire responsibility upon the Lord to take care of a problem. Actually, the Lord often desires to give *us* the wisdom to deal with our heartaches.

"We can spend our whole life trying to avoid pain. But to deny pain is to deny our humanity, and to deny that is to fall into a hidden pit of desperation, dependence, and despair. Avoiding pain becomes then our religion— negative religion, but a religion nonetheless.

"Such religion leads to desperation because we cannot avoid pain, to dependence because we soon become dependent upon those people, technologies, and faiths that promise a painless life." Finally, such beliefs lead us to "despair because sooner or later we must face pain again and again and again."[2]

Spiritual denial is a powerful belief system. Certain Christian groups and religious cults believe in the power of positive thinking to solve problems and/or claim miracles by positive confession. Some believe that evil and sickness are not real but only imaginary.

Evil and afflictions of all kinds are real. We are not immune to pain, but we don't have to suffer silently. We're to come before God with believing faith. We're to pray for healings, relief from heartaches, and for God's intervention. But we need to be open to whatever the Lord allows and put our complete faith in Him, not in the outcome we desire. God answers prayer, but He answers by His sovereign choosing.

Moreover, "death, not healing, is the great deliverance from all pain and suffering. Death delivers God's people from the hands of persecuting governments, from the ravages of disease, and from every evil affliction."[3] It's a major misconception that spiritual victory over suffering only occurs when God heals. Kate told me about when her sister Susan died of cancer:

"In my parents' minds, God's plan is to heal everyone. When Susan was diagnosed with cancer, my parents were convinced that she would be healed. But the cancer spread quickly, she was rapidly losing weight, and you could see the tumor growing in her stomach.

"The last three months my mother was taking complete care of Susan. But my parents denied the possibility that she could die even when death was around the corner.

"My cousin and a friend came from Texas to pray for Susan. Another sister called and said to me, 'It would be better if you didn't come because they're praying for healing, and you don't believe the way they do.' They didn't want anybody there with negative thoughts—only those who had total faith that Susan would be healed. They prayed that entire weekend, but on Monday she died.

"I told my mom I was upset that I didn't get to say good-bye to my sister. Mom said that she was sorry, but she didn't think Susan would die. But I'd just seen her a couple weeks before and knew she was dying.

"I felt very alone during that time, like I was on a deserted island. We could have supported each other through my sister's death. A woman in my Bible study group shared about when her daughter died. The family gathered around her and sang hymns as she was dying. That's the way it could have been when Susan died. The support, phone calls, and cards from the women in that group helped me get through my sister's death."

The Promise of Suffering

Scripture states that we will experience various trials of many kinds. "Dear friends, do not be surprised at the painful trial you are suffering, as though something strange were happening to you. But rejoice that you participate in the sufferings of Christ, so that you may be overjoyed when his glory is revealed" "So then, those who suffer according to God's will should commit themselves to their faithful Creator and continue to do good" (1 Peter 4:12-13, 19). Though this passage speaks about suffering for being a Christian, it can be applied to personal suffering as well.

If we're going to be freed from spiritual denial, we need to accept what God allows. But how do we suffer in a Christlike way?

First, we should not be surprised by or in denial about trials we suffer. "Rise to the occasion—do what the trial demands of you. It does not matter how much it hurts as long as it gives God the opportunity to manifest the life of Jesus in your body."[4]

Every loss and heartbreaking trial we go through is an opportunity for God to manifest His work in our lives and for us to demonstrate our faith in Him. We often express sorrow and at the same time testify to what the Lord is accomplishing through our heartaches. His presence can shine through us and encourage others to remain strong in faith no matter how painful the trials.

Second, when we suffer, we're not to think that something strange is happening to us. We may think that our trials are unfair and we should not have to go through them. We try to dictate to the Lord what He should do, but when He doesn't meet our demands, we're disappointed.

"Our Lord never dictated demands to His Father, and neither are we to make demands on God. We are here to submit to His will so that He may work through us what He wants. Once we realize this, He will make us broken bread and poured-out wine with which to feed and nourish others."[5]

Dave and Geri were serving as missionaries when, at the age of fifty-one, he developed a debilitating brain disease. I asked Geri if she ever asked the Lord, "Why me?" She said, "No. Bad things happen to good people all the time. Why not me? I don't feel we have nearly as much of an impact in our testimony when everything is going well."

Third, we're to rejoice that we can participate in Christ's suffering. "Are we partakers of Christ's sufferings? Are we prepared for God to stamp out our personal ambitions? Are we prepared for God to destroy our individual decisions by supernaturally transforming them? It will mean not knowing why God is taking us that way, because knowing would make us spiritually proud. We never realize at the time what God is putting us through—we go through it more or less without understanding. Then suddenly we come to a place of enlightenment, and realize—God has strengthened me, and I didn't even know it."[6]

But are we aware of when the Lord is strengthening us and meeting our needs? Are we rejoicing in the small answers, in the daily evidences of His care and supply? Are we grateful we can participate with Christ in His sufferings? He is not asking us to be thankful for evil or affliction. Never! He's asking us to rejoice in Him so He can be lifted up and honored in our suffering.

Fourth, we're to be overjoyed when His glory is revealed. "To choose God's will even though it means suffering is to suffer as Jesus did—'according to the will of God.'" The Bible never idealizes the sufferer but the glorifying of the Lord in affliction.[7]

Fifth, we're to do what is right and good even in our afflictions. "If we're going to be used by God, He will take us through a multitude of experiences that are not meant for us at all, but meant to make us useful in His hands."[8]

We need to realize the multiplied purposes of God if we're going to be useful to Him. Our heartaches are not for us alone but for others as well. The Lord desires to use us to comfort and strengthen others even as we suffer. But people can be cantankerous, difficult, and impossible. We soon realize the impossibility of ministering to others out of the goodness of our hearts. We can only serve others by the Lord's strength and goodness. When we do what is right and spiritually honoring, we can be assured of His gracious enabling power.

Scripture Reading: Mark 8:31-33

Practicing the Spiritual Life

Peter was in denial when he rebuked Jesus. What did Jesus say was wrong with Peter's viewpoint?

_____

_____

If Jesus rebuked you for being in denial and not facing reality, what do you think He would say to you?

_____

_____

For what concerns do you need to keep in mind God's interests rather than your own?

_____

_____

Prayer

"O Lord, do not rebuke me in Your anger, nor chasten me in Your hot displeasure." Those whom You love You rebuke and discipline. So I will be earnest and repent. For, Christ, You suffered many things and were rejected. You died for my sins. You were buried, and You were raised from the dead on the third day. "Oh, what joy for those whose disobedience is forgiven, whose sins are put out of sight. Yes, what joy for those whose sin is no longer counted against them by the Lord." (Ps. 6:1 NKJV not paraphrased; Rev. 3:19; Luke 17:25a KJV; 1 Cor. 15:3b, 4a NLT paraphrased; Rom. 4:7-8 NLT not paraphrased)

Prayers, Praises, and Personal Notes

_____

_____

_____

Scripture Reading: 1 Samuel 20:1-13

Practicing the Spiritual Life

About what was Jonathan in denial?

_____

_____

Though Jonathan was in denial at first, what actions did he promise to take
to help David?

_____

_____

This week make a commitment to encourage and support someone who is
hurting. Write down what you will do and when.

_____

_____

Prayer

May the Lord now show my loved ones kindness and faithfulness, and I too
will show them the same favor. Keep them safe, O God, for in You they take
refuge. "You protect them by your presence from what people plan against
them. You shelter them from evil words." May they live in the land and enjoy
security. Guide them safely so they are unafraid, but may the sea engulf their
enemies. For "the name of the Lord is a strong tower; the righteous run to
it and are safe." (2 Sam. 2:6a; Ps. 16:1 paraphrased; Ps. 31:20 NCV not paraphrased; Ps. 37:3b NRSV; Ps. 78:53 paraphrased; Prov. 18:10 not
paraphrased)

Prayers, Praises, and Personal Notes

_____

_____

_____

Scripture Reading: 2 Samuel 13:1-22

Practicing the Spiritual Life

How did Absalom's denial of Tamar's feelings of violation affect her?

_____

_____

How have you felt when someone denied the seriousness of a traumatic experience you were going through?

_____

_____

In what ways do you need comfort and help to work through and be healed of a devastating experience?

_____

_____

Prayer

O Lamb of God, "All day long my disgrace is in front of me. Shame covers my face." "I am worn out from sobbing. Every night tears drench my bed; my pillow is wet from weeping. My vision is blurred by grief; my eyes are worn out because of all my enemies. Go away, all you who do evil, for the Lord has heard my crying." "May they ever be ashamed and dismayed; may they perish in disgrace." "Have compassion on me, Lord, for I am weak. Heal me, Lord, for my body is in agony." "Heal me, O Lord, and I will be healed; save me and I will be saved, for you are the one I praise." (Ps. 44:15 GOD'S WORD; Ps. 6:6-8 NLT; Ps. 83:17; Ps. 6:2 NLT; Jer. 17:14 not paraphrased)

Prayers, Praises, and Personal Notes

_____

_____

_____

Scripture Reading: 2 Samuel 14:1-24, 28-33

Practicing the Spiritual Life

What did Joab do to get King David to face his denial about missing his son Absalom? How did David respond?

_____

_____

What did Absalom do to break through his father's denial?

_____

_____

How has the Lord helped you work through your own or others' denial?

_____

_____

Prayer

O Most High, "I have been banished from your sight." "My loved ones and my friends stand aloof from my plague, and my relatives stand afar off." "You have caused my companions to shun me; you have made me a thing of horror to them. I am shut in so that I cannot escape." "You must defend my innocence, O God, since no one else will stand up for me. You have closed their minds to understanding." Restore me, O God; make your face shine upon me that I may be saved. (Jonah 2:4a; Ps. 38:11 NKJV; Ps. 88:8 NRSV; Job 17:3-4a NLT not paraphrased; Ps. 80:3 paraphrased)

Prayers, Praises, and Personal Notes

_____

_____

_____

_____

Scripture Reading: Numbers 14:1-4, 26-30, 39-45

Practicing the Spiritual Life

How did the Israelites react in their denial after the Lord told them they could not go into the promised land?

_____

_____

In what ways can you relate to the Israelites' denial?

_____

_____

Today in what areas of your life do you need to do what the Lord desires instead of following your own ways?

_____

_____

Prayer

"There is no wisdom, no insight, no plan that can succeed against the Lord." "The Lord brings the counsel of the nations to nothing; he frustrates the plans of the peoples. The counsel of the Lord stands forever, the thoughts of his heart to all generations." Yes, Lord, "I know that you can do all things and that no plan of yours can be ruined." Therefore, I will commit my works to You, Lord, and my plans will be established. "I will hurry, without lingering, to obey your commands." (Prov. 21:30; Ps. 33:10-11 NRSV; Job 42:2 NCV not paraphrased; Prov. 16:3 NAS95 paraphrased; Ps. 119:60 NLT not paraphrased)

Prayers, Praises, and Personal Notes

_____

_____

_____

Scripture Reading: Job 5:19-27

Practicing the Spiritual Life

While denying Job's catastrophic losses, what did Eliphaz promise that God would do for Job?

_____

_____

When have others added to your grief by their denial and insensitive advice?

_____

_____

What can you learn from Eliphaz's poor example to help you be more sensitive and compassionate to those who are suffering?

_____

_____

Prayer

O ever-caring Lord, friends speak proudly every one with neighbors; with flattering lips and with a double heart they speak to me. Lord, cut off all insincere lips and the tongue that speaks hurtful things. Rise up to rescue me, as I have longed for You to do. Lord, You will keep me safe; You will always protect me from such people. "Now let your unfailing love comfort me, just as you promised me, your servant. Surround me with your tender mercies so I may live." (Ps. 12:2-3 KJV; Ps. 12:5 NLT; Ps. 12:7 NCV paraphrased; Ps. 119:76-77a NLT not paraphrased)

Prayers, Praises, and Personal Notes

_____

_____

_____

Scripture Reading: Job 19:1-3

Practicing the Spiritual Life

What did Job say to his friends about their denial of his grief and their attack on him in his suffering?

_____

_____

During what heartache have you felt the pain of having to deal with someone's denial?

_____

_____

For what trying situations do you need the Lord's support?

_____

_____

Prayer

Almighty God, "I have endured your terrors, and now I am in despair." "You have taken my loved ones and friends far away from me. Darkness is my only friend!" "Ruthless witnesses come forward. . . . They repay me evil for good and leave my soul forlorn." I am waiting patiently for You, Lord, to help me; turn to me and hear my cry. Lift me out of the pit of despair, out of the mud and the mire. Set my feet on solid ground and steady me as I walk along. (Ps. 88:15b, 18 GOD'S WORD; Ps. 35:11a-12 not paraphrased; Ps. 40:1-2 NLT paraphrased)

Prayers, Praises, and Personal Notes

_____

_____

_____

Anger and Bitterness

"Cease from anger, and forsake wrath;
Do not fret—it only causes harm."

PSALM 37:8 NKJV

*T*heresa held a responsible position in a large corporation. One day a supervisor demanded that she lie about a product the company was going to sell. That product had serious defects, which she had documented through reliable sources. When she wouldn't falsify her report, her boss put her on probation.

She was sure she would be fired so she took her report to another supervisor. It turned into a drawn-out, ugly ordeal. Eventually, her boss was fired, but by then she harbored a lot of anger and bitterness toward him.

A couple years later, she was telling a Christian friend how she felt about that boss. The friend responded, "You really hate him."

"No, I don't," Theresa answered defensively.

But as she thought about it, Theresa knew her friend was right. The hateful attitude was worse than what the boss had done. Theresa realized that her bitterness wasn't hurting him, but it was killing her.

Anger, Bitterness, and Resentment

"Almost everyone experiences anger when there is a significant loss of any kind—anger at the person who is gone, anger at people whom we think could have prevented what happened, anger at ourselves, anger at the 'system.'"[1] We can be easily offended when our emotions are raw.

Some Christians express grief by becoming angry, irritable, and even enraged. They struggle with bitterness and resentment. Others envy those who have what they want but can't obtain. For example, if they can't have children, it hurts to see a happy mother and baby. It just plain doesn't seem fair, and they're bitter!

Still others hate the way their life has changed after a loss. They hate the ordeal of dealing with the complications of a trial and necessary but unpleasant tasks. They are angry about their limitations, restrictions, and overwhelming financial expenses.

Geri struggled with anger when her husband Dave was mentally and physically incapacitated by Alzheimer's disease. "I felt angry at Dave because he was not by my side to answer questions or help me with things around the home, especially the car!

"I also became angry with God because Dave couldn't meet my need for intimacy. One night I screamed out to God as I cried and told Him I hated my body and the way He made it. It hurt to see couples holding hands or kissing each other. I angrily told the Lord that I might as well be single.

"Crying my heart out helped the healing process. I was grateful for other single women who helped me cope with life alone. The Lord took away the desires as time went on and as I began to know Him in a much deeper way through His Word."

Our anger can also be displaced in all different directions when we suffer a loss.[2] Anger can be irrational. Our sudden outrage over a small offense can shock us. We become angry over minor irritations rather than the real problem. We project our anger on other people or things instead of airing our grievances directly to the person who hurt us. We vent our anger when we're driving or take it out on a spouse, children, or pet. We get mad at someone who cuts in line in front of us at the grocery store.

"Perhaps we feel someone else is to blame for what happened: the hospital staff could have done more, and they didn't; his mother egged him into leaving; . . . she drove after drinking and caused the accident. . . . We often don't even understand why we're angry, so we need to express our frustrations in ways that do not hurt others."[3] Anger rips relationships apart when we harbor it and let it build to explosive proportions.

We have the right to be angry about others' destructive, harmful behavior. But our anger hurts others and ourselves if we don't handle the problem in a constructive way. We give people with whom we're angry power over us when our animosity toward them consumes our thoughts and emotions. Our wrath can be more harmful than the offense that provoked it. When we're consumed by anger, we lose many productive hours and even years of our lives. The Lord exhorts us: "Cease from anger, and forsake wrath; do not fret—it only causes harm" (Ps. 37:8 NKJV).

Some people also struggle with bitterness and resentment. Their loss seems so unfair; problems cannot be resolved or were unfairly settled. Often people are hurt by the insensitivity or unkindness of others.

Moreover, suffering the indignity of others' ignorance or prejudice can be especially hurtful. Many Christians who have had a loved one commit suicide or die of AIDS know the deep hurt of others' callous, cruel attitude. People who have experienced prejudice because of race, disability, or what others deem to be an inferior quality or status in life know that the feelings of bitterness, hatred, and hurt can be extremely difficult to overcome. Prejudice causes immense pain, deep wounds, and feelings of unworthiness.

Carrying the Baggage of Harmful Attitudes

When we experience a loss or a trial, our greatest heartaches most often involve others. It may be many years before we have a small measure of objectivity about the anger, bitterness, hurt, and conflicts that arose between ourselves and others. Perhaps there was very little we could have changed or done differently. We can also have regrets if we realize that we were mostly or partly to blame, were judgmental, or acted in an angry, hurtful way.

Some people brood about an unkindness and devise ways to get revenge. Others get mad and don't say anything back, but their angry silence speaks more loudly than if they'd retaliated.

We learn from our own and others' hurtful behavior by determining not to be that way, forgiving others, and becoming caring, compassionate people. But we'll never make the changes God desires of us if we continue to carry the baggage of harmful attitudes.

According to writer Gerald Sittser, "Many people are destroyed by loss because, learning what they could have been but failed to be, they choose to wallow in guilt and regret, to become bitter in spirit, or to fall into despair. While nothing they can do will reverse the loss, it is not true that there is nothing they can do to change."

Sittser explains that affliction and loss are painful enough, but the second loss—becoming an embittered, hate-filled person—doesn't need to happen. "The death that comes through loss of spouse, children, parents, health, job, marriage, childhood, or any other kind is not the worst kind of death there is. Worse still is the *death of the spirit,* the death that comes through guilt, regret, bitterness, hatred, immorality, and despair. The first kind of death happens *to* us; the second kind of death happens *in* us. It is a death we bring upon ourselves if we refuse to be transformed by the first death."[4]

This death of the spirit devastates relationships. We become resentful when we allow our minds to dwell on angry, bitter thoughts. Then others avoid us because of our self-pitying attitude. The more we feel misunderstood, the more we feel alienated and abandoned by others. On and on the hurtful cycle goes, and we become increasingly hardened.

Sittser points to a way out of this dilemma: "Our feelings do not determine what is real, though the feelings themselves are real. We cannot ignore these feelings, but neither should we indulge them. Instead, we should acknowledge them without treating them as if they were ultimate truth. The feeling self is not the center of reality. God is the center of reality."[5]

Releasing Anger, Bitterness, and Resentment

Here are some ways we can work through and release those destructive feelings of anger, bitterness, prejudice, and hatred:

First, we need to admit that we're harboring harmful attitudes. We need to accept that we are responsible for own attitudes, and others are not to blame for our feelings. We have a right to be angry at cruelty and injustice, but we can't let our animosity destroy us. We may not be able to change others or a painful situation, but we can choose to change our attitudes.

Second, we need to understand the reasons why we're holding onto harmful attitudes. Ask yourself: Why am I angry? Why am I bitter? Why am I resentful? Then write down the first thoughts that come to mind. Now read your answers and ask yourself: Are the people or situations that I'm blaming the real cause of my resentment?

"Being aware of the specific cause of anger does not involve a simple checklist, but requires some degree of self-analysis and honesty. The cause is not always other people or events; it may be personal fears, limitations, and irrational beliefs and expectations," explains counselor Mark Cosgrove.[6]

Third, we need to learn how to overcome harmful thoughts. Cosgrove points out that "problems of anger begin as seed thoughts of self-pity, discouragement, jealousy, or some other negative thought. One's thought life is the *key ingredient in behavioral and emotional control;* therefore, thoughts prior to and during times of anger are important."[7]

Fourth, we need to overcome irrational thinking. "Irrational expectations or beliefs . . . are often a refusal to accept reality because we want things to be different for our convenience or purposes."[8] We set ourselves up for deep hurt if we expect everything to go well all the time and look for others to treat us the way we want.

We need to develop a mind-set that allows us to accept that trials come from living with broken people—including ourselves. People are not perfect.

Life is not perfect; it is often unfair. Terrible things happen to us. People hurt us in thoughtless and cruel ways, and we hurt others in return.[9]

We constantly face the need to forgive others and to seek forgiveness from others. We can choose to remain stuck in anger, bitterness, and hatred; or we can choose to become people of faith, hope, and love.

Spiritual Anger, Bitterness, and Resentment

In the spiritual reaction phase, some Christians become angry with God about their afflictions or about what He desires them to do. The Lord sent Jonah to the city of Nineveh to warn the people that they would be destroyed in forty days if they didn't repent.

"When God saw what they did and how they turned from their evil ways, he had compassion and did not bring upon them the destruction he had threatened. But Jonah was greatly displeased and became angry" (Jonah 3:10, 4:1). Jonah was angry because he didn't want to obey God and go to Nineveh in the first place. Then Jonah was angry because God spared the lives of 120,000 people who were enemies of his country. Jonah became even more irrational in his anger when a vine withered up that had been shading him from the heat.

We may become spiritually angry when God leads us to serve Him in ways we don't want to or when the ministry we're involved in becomes especially hard. We can also become outraged because God allows us to suffer an injustice while serving Him, and those who committed the wrong get away with it.

Perhaps you have experienced spiritual bitterness and thought yourself oppressed by God as Job did. "I loathe my very life; therefore I will give free rein to my complaint and speak out in the bitterness of my soul. I will say to God: Do not condemn me, but tell me what charges you have against me. Does it please you to oppress me, to spurn the work of your hands, while you smile on the schemes of the wicked?" (Job 10:1-3).

Are you resentful because God has allowed your life to be filled with trouble? King Solomon said that all our days we eat in darkness and have "much sorrow and sickness and anger" (Eccl. 5:17b NKJV).

Have you been spiritually angry and bitter because you thought God had closed the hearts of others? "You have closed their minds to understanding, but do not let them triumph. God has made a mockery of me among the people; they spit in my face" (Job 17:4, 6 NLT).

Spiritual Healing of Harmful Attitudes

In 1 Peter 3:8-15 we discover principles for spiritual healing of anger, bitterness, hatred, and resentment. *First, we need to be of one mind and "have unity of spirit, sympathy, love for one another, a tender heart, and a humble mind"* (1 Peter 3:8b NRSV italics added). Christians have many differences regarding doctrine, worship, and other church matters. But the Lord calls us to be of one heart when it comes to loving one another.

"My command is this: Love each other as I have loved you" (John 15:12). As Oswald Chambers puts it, in a sense Jesus is saying:

> "I will bring a number of people around you whom you cannot respect, but you must exhibit My love to them, just as I have exhibited it to you." This kind of love is not a patronizing love for the unlovable—it is His love, and it will not be evidenced in us overnight. . . . The knowledge that God has loved me beyond all limits will compel me to go into the world to love others in the same way. I may get irritated because I have to live with an unusually difficult person. But just think how disagreeable I have been with God.[10]

Second, we're not to repay abuse with abuse or evil with evil or insult with insult. "Don't retaliate when people say unkind things about you. Instead, pay them back with a blessing. That is what God wants you to do, and he will bless you for it" (1 Peter 3:9b NLT).

Does that mean we're to subject ourselves to others' abuse and evil? No, it means that we're not to return anger with anger, or cruelty with cruelty, or prejudice with prejudice. When we retaliate against people for hurting us, we act no differently than they do. "Dear friends, never avenge yourselves. Leave that to God. For it is written, 'I will take vengeance; I will repay those who deserve it,' says the Lord" (Rom. 12:19 NLT).

How many of us harbor bitterness, hatred, and resentment and never forgive the person? It's only by the Spirit's loving power that we can release those feelings and not seek revenge. "For even Christ didn't please himself. As the Scriptures say, 'Those who insult you are also insulting me'" (Rom. 15:3 NLT).

Third, we're to pay back those who insult us with a blessing. "That is what God wants you to do, and he will bless you for it. For the Scriptures say, 'If you want a happy life and good days, keep your tongue from speaking evil, and keep your lips from telling lies. Turn away from evil and do good. Work hard at living in peace with others'" (1 Peter 3:9b-11 NLT).

We can pretend to bless others while still harboring animosity, but the

Lord sees right through us. We bless those who hurt us by being kind in return and not speaking badly of them. We bless Christians who hurt us by praying for their restoration and their spiritual well-being. We bless our enemies and evildoers by praying that they will be delivered from wrongdoing, repent, and/or come to know Jesus as their Savior. We need to pray for the personal and spiritual transformation of our enemies; then they will be the people God and we desire them to be.

Everything within us protests that it's impossible to give a blessing to someone who has been cruel or insulting. However, we can call on the life of Christ within us to do the blessing. But He can't bless anyone until *we* let go of our vengeful attitude and hatred and until we have the assurance that the Lord cares deeply about our hurt. That is the only way we can be freed from harmful attitudes that poison *all* of our relationships—not just those with people who hurt us. The most important change we can experience is the healing of our spirit and the transformation of our heart's attitude.

When we bless those who harm us, we do not give up the right to see justice done. The Lord is a God of justice and hates evil. Nor does giving a blessing minimize the seriousness of a person's wrongdoing or justify acts of abuse, prejudice, or evildoing. The harm from such acts can be deeply hurtful.

But the Lord will bless us when we bless our enemies. How? By freeing our minds and spirits from the bondage of harmful attitudes. By making us more like Him. By giving us joy and peace in the Holy Spirit. By using us to glorify Him and honor His name. By filling us with inner spiritual beauty and the light of His love.

Fourth, "*'The eyes of the Lord watch over those who do right, and his ears are open to their prayers. But the Lord turns his face against those who do evil.'* Now, who will want to harm you if you are eager to do good? But even if you suffer for doing what is right, God will reward you for it. So don't be afraid and don't worry. Instead, you must worship Christ as Lord of your life" (1 Peter 3:12-15a NLT italics added).

What comfort to know that the Lord's eyes and ears are open to our cries for justice. He opposes, frustrates, and defeats those who do evil. The Lord will heal us of our brokenness as we appropriate His peace, which is beyond all understanding and is far more wonderful than our minds can comprehend. This peace guards and protects our thoughts and emotions in Christ Jesus (Phil. 4:7).

My prayer partner, Judie, and I were trying to overcome anger, bitterness, and grief from some hurtful experiences. As we kept confessing our failure to be freed from those feelings, we felt frustrated that so much of our emotional and mental energy was consumed by hurts that could not be changed. We prayed for the ability to let go of those feelings and be at peace. Judie wrote this poem, and I kept it in my Bible and prayed it many times.

GIVE ME PEACE ANEW

Lord, You helped me through a heartache some time ago.
You gave me the answer then, but I can't seem to let it go.
The hurt was so overwhelming it can still make me cry.
Lord, I give it unto You and leave it there—at least I'll try.
Keep me from dwelling on what happened yesterday.
I'll put the pain behind me and leave it with You as I pray.
Protect me from hurtful thoughts as I bring them unto You.
I don't want to think about them; Lord, give me peace anew.[11]

Scripture Reading: Jonah 3—4

Practicing the Spiritual Life
Why was Jonah angry?

_____

_____

Try to discover the reasons why you may be harboring harmful attitudes by answering these questions: Why am I angry? Why am I bitter? Why am I resentful?

_____

_____

Now read your answers and ask yourself: Are the people or situations that I'm blaming the real cause of my feelings?

_____

_____

Prayer
O Lord of Peace, I'll get rid of my bitterness, hot temper, anger, loud quarreling, cursing, and hatred. I'll be quick to listen, slow to speak, and slow to get angry, for my anger can never make things right in Your sight. I won't sin by letting anger gain control over me. I'll think about it overnight and remain silent. I'll think about the things that are good and worthy of praise. I'll think about the things that are true and honorable and right and pure and beautiful and respected. (Eph. 4:31 GOD'S WORD; James 1:19-20 NLT; Ps. 4:4 NLT; Phil. 4:8 NCV, all paraphrased)

Prayers, Praises, and Personal Notes

_____

_____

_____

Scripture Reading: Numbers 20:1-12

Practicing the Spiritual Life

What did Moses say and do in anger? How did his anger dishonor the Lord?

_____

_____

_____

This week commit yourself to honoring the Lord by responding in a loving way rather than an angry one. Then write down how you did.

_____

_____

_____

Prayer

O God of Wisdom, "a fool gives full vent to anger, but the wise quietly holds it back." "One given to anger stirs up strife, and the hothead causes much transgression." Therefore, I will not be quickly provoked in my spirit. I will cease from anger and forsake wrath; I will not fret—it only causes harm. "Do not hide Your face from me; Do not turn Your servant away in anger; You have been my help; Do not leave me nor forsake me, O God of my salvation." For "Who is like you, O Lord, among the gods? Who is like you, majestic in holiness, awesome in splendor, doing wonders?" (Prov. 29:11, 22 NRSV not paraphrased; Eccl. 7:9a; Ps. 37:8 NKJV paraphrased; Ps. 27:9 NKJV; Ex. 15:11 NRSV not paraphrased)

Prayers, Praises, and Personal Notes

_____

_____

_____

_____

Scripture Reading: Romans 12:16-21; 1 Peter 3:8-11

Practicing the Spiritual Life

How are we to respond to insults or evil directed at us?

_____

_____

Pour your heart out writing down any insults or harmful experiences about which you harbor anger, bitterness, or hatred.

_____

_____

Copy verses or a "Prayer" from this book to help you overcome those harmful attitudes. Meditate on them daily.

_____

_____

Prayer

Lord Jesus, I am willing to listen to what You say. I will love my enemies. I will do good to those who hate me. I will pray for the happiness of those who curse me. I will pray for those who hurt me. If someone slaps me on one cheek, I will turn the other cheek. If someone demands my coat, I will offer my shirt also. I will give what I have to anyone who asks me for it; and when things are taken away from me, I won't try to get them back. I will do for others as I would like them to do for me. I will turn from evil and do good; I will seek peace and pursue it. (Luke 6:27-31 NLT; Ps. 34:14, all paraphrased)

Prayers, Praises, and Personal Notes

_____

_____

_____

Scripture Reading: 1 Peter 3:12-17

Practicing the Spiritual Life
For what does the Lord say it is better to suffer?

_____

_____

Read again what you wrote yesterday about harmful experiences. Now write statements releasing to the Lord any anger, bitterness, and hatred.

_____

_____

Write a prayer of forgiveness and blessing for each person who harmed you, including people who have passed away.

_____

_____

Prayer
Ever-forgiving Lord, do I think I deserve credit merely for loving those who love me? Even the sinners do that! And if I do good only to those who do good to me, is that so wonderful? Even sinners do that much! I will love my enemies! I will do good to them, lend to them, and not be concerned that they might not repay. Then my reward from heaven will be very great, and I will truly be acting as Your child, O Most High. For You are kind to the unthankful and to those who are wicked. I must be compassionate, just as You, Father, are compassionate. (Luke 6:32-33, 35-36 NLT, all paraphrased)

Prayers, Praises, and Personal Notes

_____

_____

_____

Scripture Reading: Job 10:1-7

Practicing the Spiritual Life

In what ways do you relate to Job's bitterness about his life and what he thought God was doing to him?

_____

_____

_____

Today what steps will you take with the Lord's help to continue overcoming bitter feelings?

_____

_____

_____

Prayer

"My complaint is still bitter today. I groan because God's heavy hand is on me." Lord, "stretch out your hand from on high; set me free." "Redeem me from human oppression, that I may keep your precepts." And I'll watch carefully so that no bitter root grows up to cause trouble and defile many. "My guilt is not hidden from you." I cannot see my own mistakes. Forgive me for my secret sins. Won't you restore my life again so that I may find joy in You? (Job 23:2 NCV; Ps. 144:7a NRSV; Ps. 119:134 NRSV not paraphrased; Heb. 12:15b paraphrased; Ps. 69:5b not paraphrased; Ps. 19:12 NCV; Ps. 85:6 GOD'S WORD paraphrased)

Prayers, Praises, and Personal Notes

_____

_____

_____

Scripture Reading: Job 17:6; 19:15-19

Practicing the Spiritual Life

In what ways were people being unkind to Job in his suffering?

_____

_____

_____

The people in Job's life show us how we should *not* treat others who are suffering. List their hurtful attitudes and actions.

_____

_____

_____

Prayer

O God, "Those who are younger than I am laugh at me." "And now they make fun of me with songs. I have become a joke to them. Since they consider me disgusting, they keep their distance from me and don't hesitate to spit in my face. Because God has untied my cord and has made me suffer, they are no longer restrained in my presence. . . . They trip my feet and then prepare ways to destroy me." "My times are in your hand; deliver me from the hand of my enemies and persecutors." "You understand, O Lord; remember me and care for me." "O Lord my God, I take refuge in you; save and deliver me from all who pursue me." (Job 30:1a, 9-11, 12b GOD'S WORD; Ps. 31:15 NRSV; Jer. 15:15a; Ps. 7:1 not paraphrased)

Prayers, Praises, and Personal Notes

_____

_____

_____

Scripture Reading: Job 27:2-4

Practicing the Spiritual Life

In what ways can you relate to Job's bitterness about his perception that God had denied him justice?

_____

_____

Despite his bitterness, what did Job say he would not do?

_____

_____

For what hurtful or unfair situation do you need the Lord's help to act and speak in a godly, truthful way?

_____

_____

Prayer

O righteous and just God, "Truth is nowhere to be found, and whoever shuns evil becomes a prey." "Furthermore, I have seen under the sun that in the place of justice there is wickedness and in the place of righteousness there is wickedness." And I am in bitterness of soul and pray to You, Lord, and weep in anguish. I will not hide Your righteousness within my heart; I will declare Your faithfulness and Your salvation. I will not conceal Your lovingkindness and Your truth from others. For "happy are those to whom the Lord imputes no iniquity, and in whose spirit there is no deceit." (Isaiah 59:15a; Eccl. 3:16 NAS95 not paraphrased; 1 Sam. 1:10 NKJV; Ps. 40:10 KJV paraphrased; Ps. 32:2 NRSV not paraphrased)

Prayers, Praises, and Personal Notes

_____

_____

_____

WEEK SEVEN

Anxiety and Fear

"For God has not given us a spirit of fear,
but of power and of love and of a sound mind."

2 TIMOTHY 1:7 NKJV

W here were you at 7:42 A.M. on October 1, 1987?"

As I walked into the foyer of Saint Joseph Hospital, I immediately saw that headline on a poster advertising earthquake preparedness workshops. I knew where I was on that date and time. I was in that hospital waiting for Ron to have a coronary angiogram.

Just as our pastor had started to pray for Ron, the entire hospital began to quake. It was terrifying as the floors and walls rolled and swayed. I panicked and wanted to run out of the building, but I was frozen in place as I held onto Ron's gurney. The quake seemed to shake forever, but it only lasted a few minutes.

The hospital in Orange County wasn't damaged, but it was close enough to the epicenter in Whittier to receive a powerful jolt. At the time the earthquake was the ninth strongest in California since 1906.

We had two earthquakes that day, both of which were terrifying. The hospital delayed medical procedures for an hour in case of aftershocks. After Ron had his test, we felt as if we'd been struck with a second earthquake. He had major arterial blockages.

Later we laughed about our pastor's powerful prayer that brought on an earthquake. But that did not diminish our anxiety and fears as Ron awaited and went through heart surgery.

Anxiety and Fear

Fear is a natural reaction when we face danger, hear threatening news, or encounter affliction. Anxiety, fear, and terror can strike us like waves of aftershocks following a major earthquake. We feel helpless, out of control, and shaken to the very core of our being. Our fears can become so intense that we feel paralyzed and wonder what is wrong with us.

The way people react in fear depends upon the kinds of trials they suffer, the severity, the complications, and the length of time these last. Someone who has a crippling or life-threatening disease, for example, feels anxious and fearful as he or she experiences emotional and physical pain and the possibility of death. Medical treatments and prescription drug side effects can be more frightening and make people more ill than the disease itself.

Symptoms of fear and anxiety include heart palpitations, pains in the chest, breathing problems, nervous stomach, nausea, vomiting, perspiring, dizziness, dry mouth, headaches, muscle tension, trembling, tingling sensations. One may become easily startled by strange sounds; have an urge to escape; feel cold, edgy, or tense, as if he or she will explode on the inside or lose control.

Anxiety is more of a generalized feeling of distress, uneasiness, or overwhelming apprehension. When we're anxious, we feel unsure about ourselves and how to handle a difficult situation. We're concerned that we'll fail in some way. Often we're not aware of our anxiety because we repress or push it away. We can suffer anxiety attacks if we keep ignoring feelings of inner distress or if our fears get out of control.

A horrifying tragedy can also cause us to suffer anxieties and fears we never had before. We feel more vulnerable and frightened by the threat of danger or possibility of another loss. We fear for our own and our loved ones' safety, whether the threat is imaginary or real. We become more guarded and try to protect ourselves from threatening situations. When we've suffered a serious loss or the death of a loved one, we may be more fearful than usual. We have lost control of our life and feel "closer to death after the loss of a significant person."[1]

Fear can be healthy or unhealthy. Ron and I lived in southern California at the time of a rash of drive-by and freeway shootings. Once Ron was driving in a *safe* neighborhood when someone from behind a block wall shot out the car window right behind his head. The police told Ron there had been random shootings in that area. Fortunately, he wasn't injured, but we were terrified by that attack. After that we were more alert to potentially dangerous situations and took safety precautions. Our fear would have been unhealthy, however, if we had been terrified every time we got in a car.

Some people repress fear so they can take care of necessary tasks and cope with complications. They push themselves, running on nervous energy. Anxiety, fear, and the energy required to deal with losses can suddenly overwhelm them and cause debilitating exhaustion.

One time a close friend received frightening, devastating news. We spent a long time together as she shared, and we cried. After a while we were exhausted from grief, but she reacted by madly cleaning her house while I fell asleep on her sofa.

How people react to fear also depends upon their personality and the way they view life. Some plan for the worst to happen in order to prepare themselves for bad news. Others are so traumatized by a loss they shut down and are paralyzed. Still others hide behind a cheerful front, acting as if all is well even though they're scared and falling apart. Then there are those people who are genuinely optimistic and face problems with a positive attitude.

"As we become aware of fear and face it, we have more freedom of choice in how we respond to it, but this requires courage. . . . Fear can discourage us. It can take the heart out of our lives and our recovery."[2]

Spiritual Anxiety and Fear

In the spiritual reaction phase, we may suffer with anxiety and fear during trials. Les Troyer was a missionary in India when he wrote about his spiritual struggles with fear. One evening he was sitting in his office with his responsibilities weighing heavily on his mind. He was also concerned about monsoon rains that always brought serious problems. Across the hall a Christian Indian woman who worked for the family was putting his three-year-old twins to bed and leading them in prayer.

Les wrote, "Suddenly, without any warning, a sharp bolt of lightning hit nearby, shaking the house and sending me straight out of my chair. I listened for screams and wails of fright from across the hallway, but only a long silence hung in the room."

Then he heard his daughter's shaky voice continue in prayer, "'And, dear Lord, if you're all alone up there tonight and you're afraid too, you just come down here and stay with us.'

"In the moment of fright and distress this child's strong faith, transcending fear, made her concerned for someone else's welfare (in this case, God's). At the same time her daddy, a veteran of years of 'walking by faith' had been brooding over fears and anxieties, robbing him of true concern, joy and happiness."[3]

How many of us would like to have the Lord come down here and personally be with us when we're scared? How many of us continue to be anxious and fearful even though we have experienced His faithfulness again and again?

Certainly, the weakest area of my personal and spiritual life has been my struggle to overcome anxiety, depression, and fear. But I am not alone. Different forms of the word *fear* appear more than 650 times in the Bible (KJV). Fear was a very real problem for the saints of Scripture.

"Fear causes the most trouble for us when we pretend we have none or when we think our lives can be totally free from fear."[4] Feeling ashamed of our anxieties and fears causes us to be discouraged and defeated. We need to keep confessing our fears to the Lord and releasing them into His hands even if we have to do it moment by moment. We need to be reassured that He understands and in His loving-kindness will help us overcome our fearfulness.

In your troubles have you seesawed between fearing God was angry with you and having the assurance that He cared about you? Job said, "His anger burns against me, and he treats me like an enemy." "Even after my skin has been destroyed, in my flesh I will see God. I will see him myself; I will see him with my very own eyes. How my heart wants that to happen!" (Job 19:11, 26-27 NCV).

Spiritually Battling Anxieties and Fears

Death, people, Satan, suffering, and tribulation are some of our major sources of fear. But freedom from those fears is not something we can gain once and for all. Battling fear is a lifetime war of *repeated overcomings* by the Holy Spirit's power and the sword of the Spirit, the Word of God.

How can we fight fear? First, we need to realize that "God has not given us a spirit of fear, but of power and of love and of a sound mind" (2 Tim. 1:7 NKJV). Our thinking is unsound when our fears are irrational. Then our "love" for the Lord and others is based on fear. God's love and sound wisdom empower us to overcome our fears and courageously deal with our heartaches.

Second, we overcome fear by accepting Jesus' love for us and holding on to Him as our security, which cannot be found in anyone or anything else. He said, "Not even a sparrow, worth only half a penny, can fall to the ground without your Father knowing it. And the very hairs on your head are all numbered. So don't be afraid; you are more valuable to him than a whole flock of sparrows" (Matt. 10:29-31 NLT).

Third, by repeatedly using Scripture, we can overcome fears that invade our minds and emotions. Memorize verses or one of the Scripture prayers in this book to help you battle fears that particularly plague you.

One of our major sources of fear is death. Facing death is never easy, but we can begin to deal with our fear of it with this promise: "Jesus said . . . 'I am the resurrection and the life. Those who believe in me, even though they die, will live, and everyone who lives and believes in me will never die'" (John 11:25-26a NRSV).

Another source of fear is people. "The Lord is with me; I will not be afraid. What can man do to me? The Lord is with me; he is my helper. I will look in triumph on my enemies. It is better to take refuge in the Lord than to trust in man" (Ps. 118:6-8).

A promise from Isaiah helps us find courage in tribulation: "But now thus says the Lord . . . Do not fear, for I have redeemed you; I have called you by name, you are mine. When you pass through the waters, I will be with you; and through the rivers, they shall not overwhelm you; when you walk through fire you shall not be burned, and the flame shall not consume you" (Isa. 43:1-2 NRSV).

We may be fearful of doing God's will. When God called Moses to deliver the Israelites from Egypt, Moses told God he was afraid, was a nobody, had a speech handicap, and finally asked God to send someone else. For every objection that Moses made, God gave a promise, and He will do the same for us. He promised, "I will be with you." "Now go; I will help you speak and will teach you what to say" (Ex. 3:12a; 4:12). We need to remember that God will be with us. He is the one who sends us. He guides us in what to say and do, and He provides others to work along with us.

During suffering, I've questioned how I could carry on doing what God desired of me. As I've been writing this book, I've experienced ongoing trials and constant interruptions. Even minor irritations have consumed my time, such as armies of ants that keep invading our kitchen.

One morning as I was having my devotions and asking the Lord how I was supposed to complete this book, He gave me this passage: "Happiness or sadness or wealth should not keep anyone from doing God's work." "In everything you do, I want you to be free from the concerns of this life" (1 Cor. 7:30, 32a NLT).

Dealing with Our Fears of Satan

"Satan attacks us individually, and we must as individuals cry out to God for help in defeating Satan as he tries to put a wedge between God and us. . . . Satan attempts to get people to curse God, to blame Him for their troubles, as well as to stop loving God."[5]

We need to understand how Satan operates so we can deal with his attacks and our fears about him. Here is how we can withstand his assaults. "Submit therefore to God. Resist the devil and he will flee from you" (James 4:7 NAS95). First, we humbly yield ourselves to the Lord and confess our need of His overcoming power. Second, we resist the devil by using Jesus' name. "All we have to say is, 'Jesus!' The need to say it cannot be overstated."[6]

Third, we need to use Scripture to withstand Satan's attacks. After Jesus' forty days of fasting in the wilderness, Satan tempted Jesus in the realm of human desires and lusts and also tried to get Jesus to worship him rather than God. The devil tempts us in those same areas. Note how Jesus resisted each temptation.

Satan urged Jesus to turn stones into bread to satisfy His hunger. "Jesus answered, 'It is written: "Man does not live on bread alone, but on every word that comes from the mouth of God"'" (Matt. 4:4; Deut. 8:3). Then Satan twisted Scripture when he quoted Psalm 91:11-12 in an attempt to test Jesus. Satan told Jesus to throw Himself off the mountain, and the angels would rescue Him. This was pure presumption and would have glorified the angels rather than Jesus. "Jesus answered him, 'It is also written: "Do not put the Lord your God to the test"'" (Matt. 4:7; Deut. 6:16).

Finally Satan took Jesus to the top of the mountain, showed him the splendor of all the kingdoms of the world, and offered them to Jesus if he would bow down and worship Satan. "Jesus said to him, 'Away from me, Satan! For it is written: "Worship the Lord your God, and serve him only"'" (Matt. 4:10; Deut. 6:13).

Through Scripture Jesus is always ready to help us and intervene on our behalf when we are tempted. "Because he himself suffered when he was tempted, he is able to help those who are being tempted" (Heb. 2:18).

Furthermore, "the most common misconceptions about Satan are that he can read your mind and that he knows the future. Every occult practice claims to know the mind (or influence it) or predict the future. But only God knows the thoughts and intents of your mind, and only He knows the future. Never ascribe the divine attributes of God to Satan."[7]

When Satan bombards our minds with vile thoughts and irrational fears, he attacks us at our point of greatest weakness. At times I have said to the enemy, "That thought was from you, and I reject it utterly. My mind belongs to the Lord, and I choose to have His thoughts, not yours. I command you to leave, in the name of the Lord Jesus Christ." Often the persistent thoughts or fears stop, although I may have to resist them again (sometimes repeatedly). Satan knows human nature, so he tries to terrify and assault us in our most vulnerable areas. He tries to bind us with fear, destroy our courage, and take away God's empowering peace. What Satan really wants to do is convince us that we cannot overcome our sins.

"Satan's traps have ensnared each of us at some spot, his prison bars have enclosed us at some moment, and his disguise as an 'angel of light' has succeeded at some point in the personal histories of each of God's flock—but Satan can show no total victory! The total victory will be Christ's."[8]

"Irrational fears compel us to act irresponsibly, or they impede us from living a responsible life. In that sense fear and faith are mutually exclusive."[9] As we overcome our fears, we are freed to lead godly, responsible lives.

God has provided victory through Christ. He has given us new natures, the mind of Christ, and the Holy Spirit's inner working, which are far more powerful than our old fearful nature. By His strength we overcome fear and stand firm in our faith even in the midst of pain and affliction. "The victory for God against Satan is when—one by one—God's people continue to love Him and trust Him in the midst of unchanging circumstances."[10]

Fear of God

The only one we are to fear and respect is God Himself. Even though Job felt God had caused his suffering, the longer Job debated with his friends, the stronger his trust in God grew. Job declared, "The fear of the Lord—that is wisdom, and to shun evil is understanding" (Job 28:28b).

"The fear of the Lord is healthy because it is the one fear that expels all other fears."[11] "Since we are receiving a kingdom that cannot be destroyed, let us be thankful and please God by worshiping him with holy fear and awe" (Heb. 12:28 NLT).

This is not the kind of fear that one has for a cruel earthly father. Our fear and respect of God draws us into His protective presence so that we may grow in godly wisdom and in our love for Him.

"And as we live in God, our love grows more perfect. So we will not be afraid on the day of judgment, but we can face him with confidence because we are like Christ here in this world. Such love has no fear because perfect love expels all fear" (1 John 4:17-18a NLT).

Scripture Reading: Job 28:28

Practicing the Spiritual Life
Why did Job believe God should be feared?

_____

_____

_____

How can proper fear and respect for the Lord give you the wisdom you need in tough times?

_____

_____

_____

Prayer
"You, O God, have heard my vows; You have given me the heritage of those who fear Your name." For the fear of You, Lord, is the beginning of wisdom; all those who practice it have a good understanding. Teach me to number my days aright that I may gain a heart of wisdom. (Ps. 61:5 NKJV not paraphrased; Ps. 111:10a NRSV; Ps. 90:12 paraphrased)

Prayers, Praises, and Personal Notes

_____

_____

_____

_____

_____

Scripture Reading: 1 John 4:14-19

Practicing the Spiritual Life

What does this passage teach us about God's love?

_____

_____

What does perfect love do?

_____

_____

What are your fears? This week ask the Lord to help you drive out those fears by His perfect love, and then write down how He helped you.

_____

_____

Prayer

O God, You have not given me a spirit of fear, but of power and of love and of a sound mind. Therefore, I will not fear, for You are with me; I will not be afraid, for You are my God; You will strengthen me; You will help me; You will uphold me with Your victorious right hand (2 Tim. 1:7 NKJV; Isa. 41:10 NRSV, all paraphrased).

Prayers, Praises, and Personal Notes

_____

_____

_____

_____

Scripture Reading: Matthew 4:1-11

Practicing the Spiritual Life

In what three ways did Satan tempt Jesus?

_____

_____

What three scriptural answers did Jesus give to refute Satan's temptations?

_____

_____

Write down and learn Scriptures you can use to stand against fears and temptations you now face.

_____

_____

Prayer

Holy Spirit, You who dwell within me are greater than the evil one who is in this world. Your blood, Jesus Christ, cleanses me from all sin. Therefore, I'll discipline myself and keep alert. Like a roaring lion my adversary the devil prowls around, looking for someone to devour. I submit myself, then, to You, O God. I resist the devil, and he must flee from me. (1 John 4:4b NKJV; 1:7b NKJV; 1 Peter 5:8 NRSV; James 4:7, all paraphrased).

Prayers, Praises, and Personal Notes

_____

_____

_____

Scripture Reading: John 11:21-27

Practicing the Spiritual Life
Who does Jesus say He is?

What promise helps us overcome the fear of death?

What hope do you have about heaven?

Prayer
Jesus, You most assuredly said to me that I who have heard Your word and believed in God who sent You have everlasting life, and I shall not come into judgment, but I have passed from death into life. Therefore, I won't let my heart be troubled. I'll trust in You, God, and I'll trust in You, Jesus. There are many rooms in Your Father's house; You would not tell me this if it were not true. You went there to prepare a place for me. Since You prepared a place for me, You will come back and take me to be with You so that I may be where You are. (John 5:24 NKJV; John 14:1-3 NCV, all paraphrased)

Prayers, Praises, and Personal Notes

Scripture Reading: Psalm 56

Practicing the Spiritual Life

Why was King David afraid of men?

_____

_____

_____

According to this psalm, what do we need to do when we're afraid of people?

_____

_____

_____

Prayer

Lord, I was in trouble, so I called to You. You answered me and set me free. I will not be afraid because You are with me. People can't do anything to hurt me. Lord, You are with me to help me, so I will see my enemies defeated. It is better to trust in You, Lord, than to trust people. It is better to trust in You than to trust princes. (Ps. 118:5-9 NCV, all paraphrased)

Prayers, Praises, and Personal Notes

_____

_____

_____

_____

_____

_____

Scripture Reading: Isaiah 43:1-2

Practicing the Spiritual Life

What promises did the Lord give the Israelites about their trials?

_____

_____

_____

Choose one of the prayers to help you overcome your fears. Write or photo-copy the prayer and offer it up to the Lord along with your fears. Then write how He helped you today.

_____

_____

_____

Prayer

O my Comforter, You are my refuge and strength, always ready to help in times of trouble. So I will not fear, even if earthquakes come and the mountains crumble into the sea. I who live in Your shelter, O Most High, will find rest in Your shadow, Almighty One. This I declare of You, Lord: You alone are my refuge, my place of safety; You are my God, and I am trusting You. You will shield me with Your wings. You will shelter me with Your feathers. Your faithful promises are my armor and protection. (Ps. 46:1-2 NLT; Ps. 91:1-2, 4 NLT, all paraphrased)

Prayers, Praises, and Personal Notes

_____

_____

_____

Scripture Reading: Exodus 3:1-14; 4:10-16

Practicing the Spiritual Life

What promises did God give Moses when Moses expressed his fears about doing God's will?

_____

_____

What fears do you have about following God's will?

_____

_____

What is God's will for you now?

_____

_____

Prayer

"Then I heard the voice of the Lord saying, 'Whom shall I send? And who will go for us?' And I said, 'Here am I. Send me!'" Teach me Your will, O Lord, and I will walk in Your truth; give me an undivided heart that I may fear Your name. "Oh, send out Your light and Your truth! Let them lead me." For You are the Lord, my God, who takes hold of my right hand and says to me, "Do not fear; I will help you." (Isa. 6:8 not paraphrased; Ps. 86:11 paraphrased; Ps. 43:3a NKJV not paraphrased; Isa. 41:13 paraphrased)

Prayers, Praises, and Personal Notes

_____

_____

_____

WEEK EIGHT

Bargaining and Depression

"Why are you downcast, O my soul?
Why so disturbed within me?
Put your hope in God,
for I will yet praise him,
my Savior and my God."

PSALM 42:11

*S*arah, a friend of mine, was diagnosed with a terminal disease. She had one request of her family and friends. She asked us to pray that she would live long enough to see her daughter Beth finish college. That prayer was answered. Sarah experienced the joy of seeing Beth graduate and start teaching kindergarten in the fall.

Bargaining

Bargaining is a way we try to postpone a loss. We ask for a favor with a deadline that we set. Bargaining often also includes the promise that we won't ask for more extensions or favors if we get what we want or if the worst is postponed.[1]

"Bargaining keeps us from facing reality, and in that way, it's a form of denial. Again, up to a point, bargaining is healthy. It protects us from a reality we're not yet ready to accept."[2] We try to prevent a painful loss by promising we'll change our attitude, do certain things, eat differently, or stop harmful habits. "Bargaining is a desperate attempt to stay in control, to have things the way we want them."[3]

Some people attempt to negotiate different kinds of bargains; if one doesn't work, they'll try another one. They bully, manipulate, or threaten others. They may become so desperate they make impossible bargains and promises they can't keep, or they continually change the conditions of their bargains or what they'll promise to do as problems grow worse.

Some people become trapped in a bargaining cycle as they make, break, and extend the deals. For example, a wife threatens her husband, "If you don't quit drinking and get help, I'll leave you."

The husband promises, "I'll stop drinking if you'll stay with me." As soon as he starts drinking again, she gives him another ultimatum, and the bargaining cycle starts over.

Other people are overwhelmed by guilt as they fail to keep their promises.

Many become angry, depressed, and/or grief stricken when their bargaining fails to prevent a loss or get them what they wanted.[4]

Trying to Bargain with God

"There are times when we verbalize our need, ask Him for help, pray for specific things, and plead with Him for a change or relief or immediate guidance, and His answer comes: 'Wait,' or 'Trust Me without a change,' or 'My grace is sufficient for you, and this is a time when I am going to answer you with My strength made perfect in your weakness, but there will be no change in the circumstances.'"[5]

If we cannot accept God's answers, however, we may try to negotiate with Him. During the spiritual reaction phase, we can get caught in a cycle of attempting to bargain with God, choosing rewards or favors, promising what we will do in return, and setting deadlines for Him to meet.

"Most bargains are made with God and are usually kept a secret" or are quietly told to a family member, friend, or pastor.[6] However, we may not be consciously aware that we are trying to bargain with God.

Some people become angry and demanding with God when they don't get what they want. When that doesn't work, they become disappointed with Him because they're certain He's not listening to them. Perhaps you can relate to Job's desperation. "Even if I summoned him and he responded, I do not believe he would give me a hearing. He would crush me with a storm and multiply my wounds for no reason" (Job 9:16-17).

Do you wish you could present your case to God and explain why you've been treated wrongfully? "Now that I have prepared my case, I know I will be vindicated. Can anyone bring charges against me? If so, I will be silent and die" (Job 13:18-19).

Have you ever thought about what you were going to pray before you prayed? You went over in your mind exactly what you would ask of God. You mentally prepared your case and the reasons why God should answer in a certain way. You felt as if you had clearly thought through all the pros and cons. It was a perfect plan, one that made good sense to you—one God would surely endorse.

You had rational arguments as to why God should do what you desired. Job said, "Surely I wish to speak to the Almighty, and I desire to argue *and* reason my case with God [that He may explain the conflict between what I believe of Him and what I see of Him]" (Job 13:3 AMP).

In desperation, we may promise to do whatever God desires of us in exchange for what we want Him to do. If God won't give us what we ask for when we're angry or demanding, then He'll give us what we need if we change our attitude and ask in a nice way.[7]

So we promise the Lord that we'll be a more faithful Christian. We'll read our Bible more, pray more, serve the Lord more. But when the crisis passes or our bargaining with God fails, we may forget the vows we made or give up in disappointment.

Depression, Hibernation, and Withdrawal

Depression is a natural grief response as we face painful losses and are forced to make unwanted changes. Depression is often stifled anger and guilt. Some people are overcome by shame and afraid they might explode in anger, so they bury their feelings and turn inward.

We can experience depression when we're sick because our emotional, mental, and physical support system normally shuts down to some degree. An impending change or loss also triggers depression, such as when a loved one has a terminal illness or an unwanted divorce is coming up.

After a serious loss or death, "we should not be surprised if we experience deep bouts of depression. We now know the permanence of our loss. We realize the extent to which our world is in shambles. We know that there is nothing we can do to make things different, and because of this we feel both hopeless and helpless."[8]

In grief we can expect to experience some or all of the following symptoms of despair and depression—desire to die, fatigue, hopelessness, low self-esteem, and suicidal thoughts. We can lose our appetite, interest in life, motivation to work, and the ability to think clearly and make decisions.[9]

Some Christians, however, claim that if we trust God, we shouldn't be depressed. Counselors such as Dr. Archibald Hart believe that it's unkind to tell those suffering grief depression to confess away their sorrow, that God doesn't want them to feel sad.

Dr. Hart points out some other misconceptions—that depression is sin, lack of faith, and that God has turned against the sufferers.[10] "They spiritualize every human problem that cannot be understood or physically seen. . . . And *only* God can cure depression, no matter how it is caused."

Hart explains that when we suffer a loss, depression is normal and will pass as we work through our grief. But depression can also be a disease caused by a chemical imbalance, a disorder of biochemistry, or other illnesses.[11] If we become crippled by depression, then we need to seek the help of a counselor and physician who specialize in treating this problem.

Along with grief depression, we may go through a period of hibernation. We need time to collect ourselves, regroup, and conserve our energy.[12] Grieving is exhausting, whether we express sorrow by crying or we don't cry at all. Survival becomes our primary focus. Being with people can be draining, and any extra activities, even ones we once enjoyed, feel like an overwhelming burden.

When we're with certain people, we may hide our true feelings to protect ourselves from being judged, misunderstood, or preached at, or to ward off sidewalk psychologists. Many Christians give well-meaning advice that misses the point or doesn't take into account the entire picture. In exasperation Job said to his friends, "I have heard many such things; miserable comforters are you all. . . . I also could talk as you do, if you were in my place; I could join words together against you, and shake my head at you" (Job 16:2, 4 NRSV).

It's critical, however, that we're not withdrawing because we're in denial and refusing to deal with reality. But if we're openly dealing with our heartaches and working through grief, then we need to protect ourselves from people who are quick to advise and condemn rather than listen with compassion and understanding.

Moreover, during this period of grief and hibernation, some people feel lethargic and can't seem to accomplish anything. Others feel apathetic and don't care if they get things done. Some try to escape by sleeping, while others suffer from insomnia. They desperately need rest, and yet they can't seem to find relief from their sorrow and the unending demands of coping with a loss.

This need for extra rest and withdrawal is a normal part of the grieving process. Setting aside times for emotional and physical restoration is essential for healing. We need to realize, however, that simply letting time pass does not heal our sorrow or solve problems. During this period of hibernation, we need to work through our grief and begin adjusting to the changes in our lives.

If we're going to recuperate from a loss, we need to determine what we absolutely must do and what we can let go of so we can get through this process. That can be very difficult when we must meet the pressing needs of family and a work schedule.

Spiritual Depression, Despair, and Withdrawal

In the spiritual reaction phase, we can be so overcome by hopelessness that we feel as if we're losing our faith and our spiritual bearings. We withdraw from the Lord because we feel shattered by the unfairness of our losses.

We struggle with depression and feel spiritually broken. In Psalm 42, the psalmist cried out three times, "Why are you downcast, O my soul? Why so disturbed within me?" (Ps. 42:5a). Then he told God why he was spiritually depressed. "My tears have been my food day and night, while men say to me all day long, 'Where is your God?'" (Ps. 42:3). It's painful enough to wonder yourself where God is. When others ask the same question about your afflictions, they confirm your deepest fear that God has abandoned you.

I know personally what spiritual depression feels like. I once reached a point of such despair that I suffered the dark night of the soul and lost all hope. I felt no sense of God's presence, went through a period of spiritual emptiness, and felt alienated from Him. I begged God to hold on to me because I had nothing left to hold on to Him. And He did. At some point I turned a corner and began to regain spiritual assurance of His tender care.

If we're going to find spiritual hope again, we need to move out of the spiritual reaction phase into the spiritual rebuilding phase. We can't do this unless we realize where we are on our pilgrimage of faith.

If it's been a couple of years since you experienced a hurtful loss, then here are some questions to consider: Are you still devastated by the permanency of your losses and hurt by what God has allowed? Are you spiritually numb? Have you put on a mask of faith? Have you turned away from God? Are you in spiritual rebellion?

Are you stuck in grief or do you feel bitter towards God? Do you dwell on or live in the past before a heartbreaking loss changed your life? You want back the *good life*, or you desperately want God to restore what you lost. Or have you created a spiritual fantasy world where you pretend your life hasn't changed? Are you living "on hold" as you wait for God to fulfill your most urgent request?

If you answered yes to any of those questions, then you're spiritually stuck. Take time to write out each question you said yes to, and then tell why you feel that way. Determine what triggered your reactions. Finally, set specific goals that will help you begin rebuilding your faith and finding hope again. You may need help from a pastor or Christian counselor in this process.

Spiritual Rebuilding

If we're going to renew our faith, we need to get through the spiritual rebuilding phase. The building up of our faith is work (not works). The effort can be hard, difficult, and even painful when our lives have been broken by senseless tragedy.

We see in Jesus' story of the wise builder and the foolish one the kind of work required. If we build our spiritual house, digging down deep and laying our foundation on the Rock, when affliction sweeps over us like a flood, our faith won't be shaken but will stand firm.

If we hear God's Word but *don't* put it into practice, it's like trying to build our faith on sand without a foundation. In one swift second when torrents of trials burst against our faith, it will collapse and crumble into ruins (Luke 6:48-49).

Continually build up your faith through Scripture, prayer, and an openness to hear the Lord speaking to you through these. Then "when the crisis comes, you will find you will stand like a rock; but if you have not been building yourself up on the word of God, you will go down, however strong your will. . . . If you are doing what Jesus told you to do, nourishing your soul on His word, you need not fear the crisis whatever it is."[13] It's not our own strength of will that keeps our faith from faltering, but our steadfast confidence in Christ and His Word.

"For no one can lay any foundation other than the one already laid, which is Jesus Christ" (1 Cor. 3:11). The spiritual house we build whose foundation is Christ must be of excellent quality, workmanship, and materials so it will stand the test. Building our faith also requires continual maintenance. It's a lifetime project, one that will never be finished until we enter heaven and occupy the house Jesus has prepared for us.

Finding Spiritual Hope

Hope is necessary to the rebuilding of our faith. "Hope is not *simply a desire or vague longing that the future will provide a sufficiency of what is lacking now.* A great deal of what is called hope in secular culture and popular religion is really wishful thinking, utopian fantasy, desire wrapped up in illusions. It is almost totally future-oriented. The time of the present is emptied of significance. . . ."[14]

Some Christians lose all hope and cannot imagine a new life with any kind of meaning or significance. But without hope faith perishes. Hope enables us to maintain spiritual strength and assurance in our Lord's ever-caring presence. But we cannot experience the healing power of hope until we realistically face our losses, accept what God has allowed, let go of what we can't have, and move forward by faith.

"The hoping person is fully aware of the harshness and losses of life. In order to hope, one must have had experiences of fearing, doubting, or despairing. Hope is generated out of a tragic sense of life; it is painfully realistic about life and the obstacles to fulfillment within and without. The Christian believer cannot simply focus on the positive in life, since there is a *cross* at the heart of Christian faith preceding any resurrection."[15]

How do we come forth from the grave of sorrow into the resurrection of hope and peace? Romans 5:1-5 takes us step by step through the process.

First, we need to realize our position in Christ. "Therefore, since we have been justified through faith, we have peace with God through our Lord Jesus Christ" (Rom. 5:1). If we're going to find hope in affliction, then we must be assured of our standing with God. Suffering does not mean He has become our enemy or that He's necessarily punishing us. When we accepted Jesus Christ as our Savior, God made us to be at peace with Him. We possess God's grace and peace because of our position in Christ.

Jesus also assured us, "I am leaving you with a gift—peace of mind and heart. And the peace I give isn't like the peace the world gives. So don't be troubled or afraid" (John 14:27 NLT).

Feeling safe is what gives us a sense of peace. Yet as hard as we or others try, we cannot give ourselves peace or security. When life brews up scary storms, we feel afraid and tense. We tell ourselves not to be so upset, but instead we become more agitated.

That's why understanding our position of peace with God is so essential. We are safe in the loving arms of Jesus. All we need to do is reach out to Him, and He will hold on to us. He will quiet our hearts and minds with His calming presence. He will undergird us with a deep inner tranquility in the darkest and deepest pain.

I have often experienced a sweet quietness of soul when my heart was broken. It was not a peace that I had given to myself; it was a gift that could only come from God. His peace abides with us always, is our comfort in sorrow, and never leaves or forsakes us even in terrifying times.

Second, "we rejoice in the hope of the glory of God" (Rom. 5:2b italics added). If we're locked into the sorrows of yesterday, we're robbed of the joy of living for the Lord today. We also miss out on the inner peace that comes with the assurance of knowing we will forever be with God in all His glory. This is cause for rejoicing and gives us a hope and a future we can count on.

Third, "we also rejoice in our sufferings, because we know that suffering produces perseverance" (Rom. 5:3 italics added). Suffering tests the genuineness of our commitment to the Lord. Our faith is trained through suffering similar to the way athletes prepare for the Olympics. They endure pain, grueling hours of exercise, and repetitious practice until their skills are perfected. Those athletes must commit years of their lives persevering toward one goal—the Olympics. Suffering produces fitness of faith and perfects us spiritually as long as we patiently persevere.

If we give up on training our faith because suffering is too grueling and painful, we miss the goal. Job said, "But God knows the way that I take, and when he has tested me, I will come out like gold" (Job 23:10 NCV). Persevering faith produces spiritual gold.

Fourth, perseverance produces character (Rom. 5:4). Endurance refines our faith and produces godly qualities. "The true expression of Christian character is not in good-doing, but in God-likeness. If the Spirit of God has transformed you within, you will exhibit divine characteristics in your life, not just good human characteristics. God's life in us expresses itself as God's life, not as human life trying to be godly."[16]

Fifth, character produces hope (Rom. 5:4). "Genuine hope enlarges the significance of the present, a present alive with possibilities. . . . Hope is not merely a longing for what we are presently missing, but rather a desire to experience more fully what we have already received."[17]

Hope appreciates what we have now and finds comfort in simple daily blessings. Hope is the steadfast assurance of the grace and peace we possess in Christ. Hope is the heart of love and the strength of faith, the assurance that God's compassion never fails. Hope always remembers this one thing—the Lord's unfailing love continues as fresh as the morning, as sure as the sunrise.

Sixth, the Holy Spirit restores our hope by pouring out God's love into our hearts (Rom. 5:5). "This hope will not disappoint us, because it is sealed with the Holy Spirit as a spirit of love."[18] As we respond to His love, ours grows deeper in return.

Finally, *"hope is the sense of possibility;* in despair and trouble, it is the sense of a way out and a destiny that goes somewhere, even if not to the specific place one had in mind."[19]

Geri and Dave Duncan were not ready to retire, but they already had some plans for their future. They wanted to travel south for the winters and take up photography again when they retired. Then at age fifty-one Dave began to experience some disturbing physical problems. He went for tests—and then more tests. The process dragged on for two years before the diagnosis came—Alzheimer's. Their dreams were shattered and their hopes for the future gone. They stood in their living room crying in each other's arms.

Suddenly, Dave stopped and said, "Enough crying, sweetheart. We have to be encouragers of others through this illness."

As Geri cared for Dave in their home for four years and then visited him in the nursing home for four more years, she watched him decline. She often felt helpless. She could do nothing to "fix" his mind or body. But remembering Dave's positive attitude kept her going.

When Dave first became ill, the Lord had given them this verse, "For I know the thoughts that I think toward you, says the Lord, thoughts of peace and not of evil, to give you a future and a hope" (Jer. 29:11 NKJV).

They had to change their view of what their future and hope would be. They realized that their future was in eternity and their hope was that Christ would use their testimony. Geri said, "That helped me focus on the task ahead of us. That task was to encourage others. It gave us something to do. We weren't going to just wait for Dave to die."

At the time Geri was Director of Prayer Ministries for Wycliffe in Oregon. This ministry was also an encouragement to her and gave her hope. She was helping others by praying for them, and that kept her focus on the Lord, where our only real hope lies.

LORD, YOU ARE MY HOPE

Lord, when I've tried everything,
and I'm at the end of my rope,
I'll not fear what lies before me,
for You are my hope.
When I don't know which way to go,
and in the darkness I grope,
I'll trust You to lead me step by step,
for You are my hope.
When my problems overwhelm me,
and I wonder how I'll cope,
I'll remember the promises in Your Word,
and in them I'll put my hope.[20]

Scripture Reading: Psalm 42

Practicing the Spiritual Life

In what ways can you relate to the psalmist in his spiritual depression?

_____

_____

_____

Every day this week write down how you find hope in the Lord, and praise Him for the ways you have been encouraged.

_____

_____

_____

Prayer

Lord God, "I stretch out my hands to you in prayer. Like parched land, my soul thirsts for you." "I am bowed down and brought very low; all day long I go about mourning." "The Lord has forsaken me, my Lord has forgotten me." "But God, who comforts the downcast, comforted us." "You are the God who saves me. All day long I put my hope in you." "With my mouth I will give thanks abundantly to the Lord; and in the midst of many I will praise Him." (Ps. 143:6 GOD'S WORD; Ps. 38:6; Isa. 49:14b NRSV; 2 Cor. 7:6a; Ps. 25:5b NLT; Ps. 109:30 NAS95 not paraphrased)

Prayers, Praises, and Personal Notes

_____

_____

_____

_____

_____

Scripture Reading: Romans 5:1-5

Practicing the Spiritual Life

What do we have in God through Christ, and in what can we rejoice?

_____

_____

_____

What attitudes and actions do you need to change so that trials can produce perseverance, character, and hope?

_____

_____

_____

Prayer

May Your unfailing love rest upon me, O Lord, even as I put my hope in You. Your divine power has given me everything I need for life and godliness through my knowledge of You who called me by Your own glory and goodness. For this very reason, I will make every effort to add to my faith goodness; and to goodness, knowledge; and to knowledge, self-control; and to self-control, perseverance; and to perseverance, godliness. Godliness leads me to love other Christians, and finally I will grow to have genuine love for everyone. The more I grow like this, the more I will become productive and useful in my knowledge of You, Lord Jesus Christ. (Ps. 33:22; 2 Peter 1:3, 5-8 NLT, all paraphrased)

Prayers, Praises, and Personal Notes

_____

_____

_____

Scripture Reading: Jeremiah 29:11; Hebrews 10:22-23

Practicing the Spiritual Life

What kind of plans does the Lord have for us?

_____

_____

How are we to draw near to God, and what are we to hold onto?

_____

_____

Even if you are going through trying times, in what way will you be an encouragement and bring hope to someone else?

_____

_____

Prayer

Lord, Your plans stand firm forever. Your thoughts stand firm in every generation. Therefore, I will know and serve You with a single mind and willing heart, for You search my mind and understand my every plan and thought. Surely, Lord, I have a future ahead of me; my hope will not be disappointed. I know also that wisdom is sweet to my soul; if I find it, there is a future hope for me, and my hope will not be cut off. "I will praise you forever for what you have done; in your name I will hope, for your name is good. I will praise you in the presence of your saints." (Ps. 33:11 GOD'S WORD; 1 Chron. 28:9a NRSV; Prov. 23:18 NLT; Prov. 24:14 paraphrased; Ps. 52:9 not paraphrased)

Prayers, Praises, and Personal Notes

_____

_____

_____

Scripture Reading: Job 9:14-20

Practicing the Spiritual Life

How did Job think God would respond if he tried to bargain with Him?

_____

_____

_____

About what have you tried to bargain with God?

_____

_____

_____

Prayer

"I cry out to you, O God, but you do not answer; I stand up, but you merely look at me." "Why do you hide your face and forget our misery and oppression?" "O Lord, hear my prayer, listen to my cry for mercy; in your faithfulness and righteousness come to my relief." For "Your righteousness is like the mighty mountains, your justice like the ocean depths." "Keep back Your servant also from presumptuous sins; let them not have dominion over me. Then I shall be blameless, and I shall be innocent of great transgression." (Job 30:20; Ps. 44:24; Ps. 143:1; Ps. 36:6a NLT; Ps. 19:13 NKJV not paraphrased)

Prayers, Praises, and Personal Notes

_____

_____

_____

_____

_____

Scripture Reading: Job 13:17-19; 23:4-7

Practicing the Spiritual Life

What did Job prepare so he could present his arguments and bargain with God?

_____

_____

What did Job think God would do for him?

_____

_____

During what trials have you given God reasons why He should answer you in a certain way?

_____

_____

Prayer

Merciful Lord, "You have heard my voice: 'Do not hide Your ear from my sighing, from my cry for help.' You drew near on the day I called on You, and said, 'Do not fear!' O Lord, You have pleaded the case for my soul; You have redeemed my life. O Lord, You have seen how I am wronged; judge my case." "Stir up Yourself, and awake to my vindication, to my cause, my God and my Lord." "Let those who desire my vindication shout for joy and be glad, and say evermore, 'Great is the Lord, who delights in the welfare of his servant.'" (Lam. 3:56-59 NKJV; Ps. 35:23 NKJV; Ps. 35:27 NRSV not paraphrased)

Prayers, Praises, and Personal Notes

_____

_____

_____

Scripture Reading: Isaiah 38; 2 Chronicles 32:24-26

Practicing the Spiritual Life

What did King Hezekiah ask for when he bargained with the Lord, and how did God answer?

_____

_____

_____

How are Hezekiah's bargaining and the promises he made to God an example of what we should and should not do?

_____

_____

_____

Prayer

Remember me, O Lord; do not be exceedingly angry, and do not remember my iniquity forever. "What gain is there in my destruction, in my going down into the pit? Will the dust praise you? Will it proclaim your faithfulness?" "It is better to be of a lowly spirit among the poor than to divide the spoil with the proud." "I will be glad and rejoice in your love, for you saw my affliction and knew the anguish of my soul." I fear You, Lord, and will serve You in truth with all my heart; for I have considered what great things You have done for me. (Isa. 64:9a NRSV paraphrased; Ps. 30:9; Prov. 16:19 NRSV; Ps. 31:7 not paraphrased; 1 Sam. 12:24 NKJV paraphrased)

Prayers, Praises, and Personal Notes

_____

_____

_____

Scripture Reading: Job 10:18-22

Practicing the Spiritual Life

In his despair and depression, what did Job wish had happened to him?

_____

_____

Were you ever so depressed that you wondered why you were born or questioned God's purposes for your life? If so, explain.

_____

_____

What encouragement and hope do you find in the prayer below regarding your birth and your life?

_____

_____

Prayer

Creator of Life, "Your hands shaped and made me. Do you now turn around and destroy me? Remember that you molded me like a piece of clay. Will you now turn me back into dust?" "You made all the delicate, inner parts of my body and knit me together in my mother's womb." "You watched me as I was being formed in utter seclusion, as I was woven together in the dark of the womb." "You dressed me with skin and flesh; you sewed me together with bones and muscles. You gave me life and showed me kindness, and in your care you watched over my life." (Job 10:8-9 NCV; Ps. 139:13, 15 NLT; Job 10:11-12 NCV not paraphrased)

Prayers, Praises, and Personal Notes

_____

_____

_____

WEEK NINE

Secure in God's Forgiveness

"If we confess our sins,
He is faithful and just to forgive us our sins
and to cleanse us from all unrighteousness."

1 JOHN 1:9 NKJV

*C*raig Nimmo was a missionary and airplane maintenance engineer in Papua New Guinea. It was almost dinnertime, and two planes were due back before dark. Craig had just gotten home from work when the phone rang. He was hit cold with the news that the Aztec plane he'd just worked on had crashed, and seven people perished instantly.

Craig said, "I was too stupefied to feel emotion. I stumbled off in a daze. My thoughts ran around in tortured circles. . . . The events of the preceding two days had been routine. We'd pulled a 100-hour inspection on the Aztec. . . . My main job was inspecting the right engine, the one that caught fire."

While Craig was working on the engine, another mechanic had asked him for help. He had just hooked up the fuel line and twisted the B-nut finger-tight, but he needed to finish tightening the nut with a wrench. After helping his coworker, he forgot that final step.

Craig said, "The lack of a final twist of the wrench on that fuel line meant a fine spray of gasoline could escape. It went unnoticed on the post-inspection run-up, but after several hours of flying, the nut must have loosened more, and then . . . WHOOSH! Fire!" A later inspection of the plane proved what Craig had feared. "My failure to tighten that nut cost seven people—my close friends and coworkers—their lives.

"The funeral was a ghastly ordeal. The sight of those caskets lined up in the little open-sided tropical church hit me like a blow to the stomach. . . . Oblivious to anything but my grief, I was absolutely, totally wretched. How could I face my friends? How could I face myself? I was overwhelmed by guilt. . . . The tyranny of that failure made the next few days the worst I've ever endured."

Craig wanted to talk with Glennis, the wife of Doug, the pilot who had died, but he was afraid. "What would she say? I couldn't face her, so I put it off. And the longer I put it off, the harder it got."

On the day Doug's oldest daughter and his brother were scheduled to return home, Craig felt the Lord was telling him to talk to them. He went into the pilots' lounge where they were waiting and asked everyone but the family to leave the room. After the others left, Craig said, "I closed the door and opened my broken heart. I wept and wept. My voice choked with sobs. I asked their forgiveness.

"'That hand there,' I said, as I held out my quivering right hand, 'took Doug's life.' Almost incoherent, sobs shaking my whole body, I sat wrapped in misery. Glennis reached out to take my hand in both of hers, the hand that took her husband's life. The warmth of her love and forgiveness flowed over my aching heart like a balm. On the other side Doug's brother sat with his arm around me.

"It was the most significant first step in the healing process that was to be my experience over the next few years. In the warmth of their forgiveness, the cloak of misery I clutched so tightly began slowly to drop away.

"And that wasn't all. I knew forgiveness from everyone around me—my coworkers and, most importantly, the pilots who continued to entrust themselves to my skill and workmanship. . . . I could've been the failure I thought I was. But for God's grace, I'd be somewhere cowering in a corner in guilt-ridden despair—the eighth fatality of the Aztec crash. That would *really* be failure."[1]

Guilt, Shame, and Self-Blame

Bearing the consequences of our failure can be extremely painful. It's sadly true that most of our suffering and sorrow are a result of our own and others' sins, either directly or indirectly due to living in a fallen world. But if you have ever experienced serious failures or wrongdoing, you can become a personal and spiritual fatality if you give up in guilt-ridden despair. You can be destroyed by failure if you can't accept God's healing grace and everlasting forgiveness, which are already yours.

In the spiritual reaction phase, feelings of guilt, shame, and self-blame are normal when people are grieving over a failure, loss, or other heartache. Some people feel shame because they're going through a series of hard trials. They're embarrassed that they have so many needs and problems. Others are ashamed that they or a loved one have a disease, chronic illness, or handicap. If a family member commits a crime, his or her destructive actions can bring shame on an entire family.

When we experience a loss, we can get caught up in the if onlys—*if only*

I had done this or that, said this or hadn't said that. If only I'd been there, it wouldn't have happened. We blame ourselves even if we did everything we could or if there was nothing we could have done.

We often feel guilty when a loved one dies, a relationship is broken, or we lose a job. We think that if we had done more or tried harder, we could have changed the outcome. Perhaps we realize too late that we could have handled things differently.

According to Dr. Elizabeth Harper Neeld:

> Since no human being is perfect, it will be highly unlikely that we do not feel guilty about something related to the lost person: . . . we had thoughts we are now ashamed of; we have mixed feelings about our relationship with the lost person; we hurt the person unnecessarily; . . . and the list goes on. . . . The important thing at this point in the grieving process is to withhold final judgment about these matters until we are under less stress and can think more clearly. We should hold out the possibility at least that our judgment of ourselves may be more harsh than is warranted.[2]

Spiritual Struggles with Guilt and Shame

Have you ever felt undeserving of God's love? Have you asked, "How can a holy God love me when I sin constantly and daily? When I sin deliberately? When I sin and confess and repent and then commit the same sin again?" If your life has been broken by destructive choices, you wonder how to live with the painful consequences. How can the Lord possibly forgive?

Larry Weeden wrote in his book *Feeling Guilty, Finding Grace:* "Many Christians, if not most, are constantly weighed down with guilty feelings. . . . What are the sources of these feelings that plague our existence day in, day out, robbing us of the abundant life Jesus intends for us to experience?"[3] How does guilt and shame cause us to become spiritually stuck, prevent us from working through the healing process, and rob us of the joy of our salvation?

An addictive and habitual pattern of sin causes guilt, shame, and spiritual defeat. Such sins ought to cause us to feel guilty. "That's genuine guilt produced by the indwelling Holy Spirit that is meant to drive us back into God's loving, forgiving arms. . . . Whatever our areas of frequent defeat, the plain fact is that until we begin to make substantial progress in them, we're going to feel guilty *as we should,* because we are guilty of those fresh offenses against God's holiness. . . . We don't have to go on living in defeat and guilty misery. We can begin to make steady progress in overcoming sinful habits."[4]

But we can become so overwhelmed by self-condemnation that we hinder our own spiritual progress and the Holy Spirit from delivering us from sin and renewing our lives. The only way to be relieved of guilt is to repent and do everything we can by God's power to overcome our sin. For addictive or habitual sin, we may need the help of a godly friend, pastor, or counselor.

We need to be assured that when we repent, through Christ the Savior we are forgiven. "If we confess our sins, He is faithful and just to forgive us our sins and to cleanse us from all unrighteousness" (1 John 1:9 NKJV). When Jesus died on the cross, He took all our sins on Himself, paying the price we should have paid. The power of the cross is greater than the power of all our sin, guilt, and shame.

Overcoming sin is an ongoing process. As we work in partnership with the indwelling Holy Spirit to be freed from harmful attitudes and actions, we experience the blessing of seeing our hearts and lives transformed. "Repent, then, and turn to God, so that your sins may be wiped out, that times of refreshing may come from the Lord" (Acts 3:19).

However, false guilt and shame over offenses already confessed can cause us to become spiritually stuck. We repented and made the necessary changes in our behavior. "We asked for forgiveness from those we hurt, and we made amends. Yet despite having done those things, we still feel guilty. We may have confessed it and asked for God's cleansing over and over, literally hundreds of times in some cases."[5]

We can be crippled by false guilt if we're convinced that God hasn't forgiven us. Satan, the father of lies and affliction, falsely accuses us in our thoughts, telling us that we are guilty or that God has caused our suffering.

Forgiving Ourselves and Others

"Sin often has results that stay with us for years, perhaps even for the rest of our lives. The results may be physical, emotional, spiritual, or some combination of the three. And they serve as reminders that can bring on fresh waves of guilty feelings every time we encounter them."[6]

A woman named Ruth tells about her eleven-year struggle to find spiritual healing. "On January 15, 1977, I had an abortion. The silent pain I felt is hard to describe. But it changed my life forever. A part of me died. I have never felt so alone as I did that day. I was alone with no one to hold my hand or say they loved me. I sat silently with twenty other young girls and women waiting their turn.

"Later as I tried to go on with my life and serve God, all the while acting as though nothing was wrong, I held onto my secret. I grieved for my little one. Silently. Silently, alone. Later that year I was married to the father of our unborn child, but that didn't heal my broken heart.

"People would ask me, 'When are you having children?'

"'I don't know—in a few years,' I'd answer.

"But inside I thought, *I don't deserve a child*. When I saw babies, my heart ached. I always wanted to have four sons because I had brothers, but I felt, *No, I don't deserve a son*.

"Not only was the experience itself painful, but before the abortion there were the months of lies and sneaking around. Mom told me many times that if I disobeyed my parents either doing something that they told me not to do or that my common sense disapproved of, I would open myself to temptation. She called it my umbrella of protection. When I disobeyed, I was stepping out from under my umbrella.

"I had a strong Christian upbringing, so I knew what was right and wrong. I can still pinpoint the day I stepped out from under my umbrella. It was raining pretty hard, and the temptation to give myself to my future husband overcame me.

"Many times I asked the Lord to forgive me for having sex outside of marriage, for the abortion, and to help me to live for Him. He always held up His end of it. I, on the other hand, had trouble really understanding what God meant when He said He forgives and forgets. I didn't and couldn't forgive myself.

"God touched me many times with His love and showed me in new ways that He cared for me. But my silent pain put conditions on His love. I always told myself that the pain I felt was a consequence of my sin. Many years passed as God kept showing me how much He loved me. For example, my husband and I have three children. God showed me little miracles and big ones.

"Unknowingly, all that time I was trying to make my husband, whom I love very much, pay a debt he could never pay for the pain I felt about the abortion. It was through my close friend and sister-in-law that God spoke to me about my attitude toward my husband. She was sensitive to the Holy Spirit's leading and wrote me a letter that was painful to read.

"She told me I was hurting my husband because of my own guilt and by not forgiving him. His debt to me was so great he could not possibly pay it.

It was destroying him and me and our relationship. She told me I should forgive and accept God's unconditional forgiveness for me. I prayed for God to speak to me because if that was the truth, then I wanted to let Him change me and help me forgive myself and my husband.

"Out of obedience, I asked God to change me even though I didn't feel like it. I also counseled with our pastor whom God used to help me through the healing process. Over a period of several months, God ministered to and spoke to me in many different ways to help me forgive.

"The Holy Spirit did change my heart. He performed a miracle in me and healed me. God gave me the ability to forgive myself and my husband and to release him from a debt I felt he owed me. Our marriage was restored, and we renewed our wedding vows before our church congregation. Finally, my grieving was over, and in our hearts our little one was laid to rest.

"The Lord turned my silent pain into a glorious testimony of His power to do more than we can even think or imagine. I've been surprised that God could bring good out of the pain of what I did wrong. Since then I have had many opportunities to share my testimony, and the Lord has used me to help other women. I've been able to share with them how I found God's forgiveness and healing."

Like Ruth, many of us are haunted by guilt for years after committing a wrong. We dare not ignore this guilt and the sin that caused it. "It's vital that we remember our faults because only then can we do the real work of forgiving ourselves. Only by bringing things into the open can we deal with them."[7]

Dealing with Guilt and Sin

"One of the most common ways of avoiding guilt is to stuff it, to try to ignore it. That's called *repression*. Sometimes for brief periods, we do try to deal honestly with our sins before God. But then, because we still don't feel forgiven, we quickly try to hide from it again. At other times, we repress all thought of our guilt for as long as possible and hope against hope that we'll never have to confront it directly."[8]

In addition, some people take little or no responsibility for their repeated failures and wrongdoing. They continue in a habitual pattern of being irresponsible and hurting others while minimizing the impact of their own harmful behavior. They often in fact claim to be the victims. Everyone else is wrong or caused their problems.

Others not only repress guilt, but they are in complete denial about their harmful behavior. They lead deceitful, hurtful, and/or immoral lives while pretending to be morally and spiritually righteous. They condemn others for failures and sins while covering up their own. The more hardened they become to their own ongoing pattern of sin, the more self-righteous and condemning they become of others.

People who lead such double lives often think their sins are hidden—they even try to hide them from themselves. But eventually God exposes their self-deceit. They usually break down when they can no longer maintain their spiritual pretense. Then they may walk away from their faith in bitterness while blaming others for their fall.

We need to be honest with ourselves about our sin because we "have an amazing capacity to repress the truth about ourselves and justify even our worst behaviors. We can do awful things and yet convince ourselves, even as we're doing them, that our words and actions are good and proper," writes Larry Weeden in *Feeling Guilty, Finding Grace*. "Another way we try to get around our guilt is called *projection* or blame shifting." We believe our wrongdoing is minor compared to what others have done to us.

Weeden continues, "Ultimately, we're tempted to blame God Himself for our failures. We don't give voice to the thoughts, of course, because we're afraid of being irreverent or of how God would react." We're torn between our own failure and our frustration with God for not doing for us what we cannot seem to do for ourselves. "Indeed, even as we blame God," says Weeden, "a part of us still knows we're responsible for our own choices, which leads to even more guilty feelings."[9]

God, of course, is not to blame. We are accountable to Him for all of our actions. Satan is the one who constantly tempts us, accuses us, and tries to defeat us with shameful thoughts and the desire to give into temptation.

Overcoming sin and hurtful attitudes and actions is a process—not an instantaneous deliverance, particularly when it comes to addictive, habitual sins. A few people quickly overcome an addiction, but most fall and fall again as they continue to battle particular sins. Even after people stop drinking, using drugs, or whatever sin held them captive, it's a moment-by-moment choice to abstain from addictive behaviors.

We need to deal honestly with our sins and realize the healing power of God's forgiveness. "His embrace *and knowing in our deepest heart that we are forgiven and accepted* begins with bringing our sins into the open before Him in humble yet expectant prayer. In addition, we will only be able to forgive *ourselves* when we're this honest about what we've done."[10]

If we're going to find healing, we need to deal honestly with the following questions:

Am I experiencing guilt? If so, write down those things about which you feel guilty. Ask the Lord to show you if your guilt is false or genuine.

Am I suffering from feelings of failure because of sins I can't seem to overcome? Am I blaming others? If so, why?

Am I living a secret life of sin and fearful I will be discovered? If so, write down your secrets; they need to be brought out into the light.

Am I willing to repent of those sins, turn away from them, and turn back to the Lord? If so, what specific actions will I take to overcome those sins? To whom will I be accountable to follow through?

This is a painful but healing process. It's essential to realize that you will hinder your progress in overcoming sin if you keep putting yourself down or dwelling on feelings of shame, such as: *I'm so terrible the Lord can't help me. He will never forgive me for what I've done wrong.*

Hurtful self-talk will discourage you and hinder your progress. Satan also attacks us by trying to make us feel bad about ourselves. His sole purpose is to defeat us by convincing us that we're such failures God can never restore us.

Your life can be a total wreck. You can be in such deep trouble that you see no hope of ever getting out of it. You may not be able to imagine the Lord forgiving you for what you've done wrong. You may have committed a serious crime, abused someone cruelly, or even taken someone's life. Society or the victims or their loved ones may consider your deed unforgivable. But if you genuinely confess your sin, turn from your evil way of life, and accept Christ as Savior, He will forgive you. You must cling to the belief that the Lord loves you, will deliver you from sin, transform your life, and accept you into heaven. Nothing, absolutely nothing, is impossible with the Lord—even you.

When you fall, get up. Repent and ask the Lord for forgiveness and to free you from guilt and shame. Never give up! The Lord can restore and renew your life in ways beyond your hopes and imagination.

"The bottom line: If we'll pause to think about it in the light of God's truth, we have no reason to hide from Him, regardless of how or how often we've sinned, and every reason to come to Him in honest confession and repentance. We can return to our Father to bare our souls again and again—as often as necessary—knowing we *will* find compassion, understanding, and forgiveness."[11]

How many times will God forgive us? Remember the question Peter asked Jesus? "'Lord, how often shall my brother sin against me, and I forgive him? Up to seven times?' Jesus said to him, 'I do not say to you, up to seven times, but up to seventy times seven'" (Matt. 18:21-22 NKJV). If Jesus told Peter to forgive 490 times—which is only an example and not the limit—will the Lord not forgive us even more?

Forgiving the Unforgivable

Some wrongdoing seems humanly unforgivable. How can you say to parents whose child has been abducted and never found that they should be forgiving? What about a brutalized rape victim? What about a person who has been subjected to a childhood of abuse or neglect? What about a spouse who leaves a family destitute and refuses to support them? What about those whose loved one was murdered?

We daily see on television heartbreaking acts of crime and violence. In a nearby city, a mother was entering a credit union when a bank robber shot and killed her in front of her young son. Until you've experienced such a tragedy, you can't begin to understand the anguish of such a loss.

Yet the only way people find personal healing at these times is to give up the desire for revenge, the hatred, and the inability to forgive. That's not easy to say to someone who has experienced serious harm. Those who have lost a loved one in such a way endure a lifetime of sorrow.

People still need to come to the point of reconciling themselves to the fact that a painful loss cannot be undone. If they carry the weight of unforgiveness, they become embittered. If they're going to grow through their grief, they need to forgive, by God's tender grace, and put the offender in the hands of God, who is just and fair.

Though justice may not be done here, ultimately those who committed such wrongs will be accountable to God. The only way people will ever be able to extend forgiveness to those who caused harm is to deal with a truth that is avoided and feared by Christians—God's judgment and hell as the final place of punishment for the wicked.

Believing this truth can actually be a comfort and relief to those who are so angry they feel it's impossible to forgive some horrible offense. "Beloved, do not avenge yourselves, but rather give place to wrath; for it is written, 'Vengeance is Mine, I will repay,'" says the Lord" (Rom. 12:19 NKJV).

Be assured, at the end of the age, "The Son of Man will send out his angels, and they will weed out of his kingdom everything that causes sin and all who do evil. They will throw them into the fiery furnace, where there will be weeping and gnashing of teeth. Then the righteous will shine like the sun in the kingdom of their Father" (Matt. 13:41-43a). We can be grateful that God alone is the Judge who determines the eternal destiny of each person.

We must believe that the Lord who has promised we will be free from sin and sorrow in heaven will totally heal us of all pain suffered from the harm caused by others. We have this heavenly hope to look forward to. "No longer will violence be heard in your land, nor ruin or destruction within your borders, but you will call your walls Salvation and your gates Praise. . . . Your sun will never set again, and your moon will wane no more; the Lord will be your everlasting light, and your days of sorrow will end" (Isaiah 60:18, 20).

Scripture Reading: Psalms 103:8-12

Practicing the Spiritual Life

How far has the Lord removed our sins and transgressions from us?

_____

_____

How great is God's love for us?

_____

_____

In what ways do you personally find assurance in God's promises?

_____

_____

Prayer

Ever-forgiving Savior, I acknowledge my sin to You and will not hide my iniquity. I will confess my transgressions to You, Lord; forgive the guilt of my sin. Help me, O God of my salvation, for the glory of Your name; deliver me and forgive my sins for Your name's sake. For You, O Lord, are a God merciful and gracious, slow to anger and abounding in steadfast love and faithfulness. You take pleasure in those who fear You, in those who hope in Your steadfast love. (Ps. 32:5; Ps. 79:9; Ps. 86:15; Ps. 147:11 all NRSV, all paraphrased)

Prayers, Praises, and Personal Notes

_____

_____

_____

_____

_____

Scripture Reading: Job 10:14-17

Practicing the Spiritual Life

What did Job think God was doing to him as he struggled with false shame over his affliction and losses?

_____

_____

About what have you felt shame?

_____

_____

Find Scriptures or a "Prayer" from this book to help you overcome feelings of shame. Daily meditate on them.

_____

_____

Prayer

Ever-loving Lord, "Even if I were right, my own mouth would say I was wrong; if I were innocent, my mouth would say I was guilty." "Correct me, Lord, but only with justice—not in your anger, lest you reduce me to nothing." "I hold fast to your statutes, O Lord; do not let me be put to shame." "I have taken refuge in you, O Lord. Never let me be put to shame. Save me because of your righteousness." Restore me to Yourself, O Lord, that I may be restored; renew my days as of old. (Job 9:20 NCV; Jer. 10:24; Ps. 119:31; Ps. 31:1 GOD'S WORD not paraphrased; Lam. 5:21 NRSV paraphrased)

Prayers, Praises, and Personal Notes

_____

_____

_____

Scripture Reading: Luke 7:37-50

Practicing the Spiritual Life

How did Jesus respond to the woman who so openly sought forgiveness for her many sins?

_____

_____

In what ways do you relate to this woman's need for forgiveness?

_____

_____

What hope do you find that your life can be changed and that Jesus will forgive you?

_____

_____

Prayer

"For the sake of your name, O Lord, forgive my iniquity, though it is great." For I desire to live according to my new life in the Holy Spirit. Then I won't be doing what my sinful nature craves. My old sinful nature loves to do evil, which is just the opposite to what You, Holy Spirit, want. And You give me desires that are opposite to what my sinful nature desires. These two forces are constantly fighting each other, and my choices are never free from this conflict. "But You, O God the Lord, deal with me for Your name's sake; because Your mercy is good, deliver me" (Ps. 25:11 not paraphrased; Gal. 5:16-17 NLT paraphrased; Ps. 109:21 NKJV not paraphrased)

Prayers, Praises, and Personal Notes

_____

_____

_____

Scripture Reading: 1 John 1:5-10

Practicing the Spiritual Life

What are the differences between walking in the light and in darkness?

_____

_____

When we confess and repent of our sins, what do we experience?

_____

_____

If you're in denial about certain sins or claiming they're not serious, what steps will you take to face them and repent?

_____

_____

Prayer

Jesus, You are the light of the world. If I follow You, I won't be stumbling through the darkness, because I will have the light that leads to life. I repent now and turn to You, God, so that my sins may be wiped out, that times of refreshing may come from You. I will do what is right and come to the light gladly, so everyone can see that I am doing what You want. For, Jesus, You gave Your life to free me from every kind of sin, to cleanse me, and to make me Your very own, totally committed to doing what is right. (John 8:12 NLT; Acts 3:19; John 3:21 NLT; Titus 2:14 NLT, all paraphrased)

Prayers, Praises, and Personal Notes

_____

_____

_____

_____

Scripture Reading: 2 Samuel 12:1-14

Practicing the Spiritual Life

What "secret" sins did King David commit? What were the consequences?

_____

_____

_____

If you have secret sins, how will you be accountable to the Lord and a trust-worthy Christian to overcome those sins, make necessary changes, and do what is right?

_____

_____

_____

Prayer

Ever-forgiving Savior, "Wash away all my guilt and make me clean again." "For I recognize my shameful deeds—they haunt me day and night." "You spread out our sins before you—our secret sins—and you see them all." "You are the only one I have sinned against; I have done what you say is wrong. You are right when you speak and fair when you judge." "You want me to be completely truthful, so teach me wisdom. Take away my sin, and I will be clean. Wash me, and I will be whiter than snow." (Ps. 51:2 NCV; Ps. 51:3 NLT; Ps. 90:8 NLT; Ps. 51:4, 6-7 NCV not paraphrased)

Prayers, Praises, and Personal Notes

_____

_____

_____

Scripture Reading: Matthew 18:21-22; Luke 6:37; Ephesians 4:32

How often are we to forgive others and why?

List some ways you have been wronged. Write statements forgiving the person or persons responsible.

Write a prayer acknowledging that the Lord is the Judge and asking Him to heal you of your hurt.

Prayer

O God, as Your chosen one, holy and beloved, I will clothe myself with compassion, tenderhearted mercy, kindness, humility, gentleness, and patience. I will bear with and make allowances for others' faults and forgive those who offended me; just as You, Lord, have forgiven me, so I also will forgive. Above all, I will clothe myself with love, which binds everything together in perfect harmony. (Col. 3:12-13 NRSV, NLT; 3:14 NRSV, all paraphrased)

Prayers, Praises, and Personal Notes

Scripture Reading: Job 9:27-31

Practicing the Spiritual Life

Job had false guilt because his suffering was not due to his sins. Why did Job feel hopeless as he struggled with guilt feelings?

_____

_____

_____

When have you struggled with false guilt over sins that you've repented of, questioning if God had forgiven you?

_____

_____

_____

Prayer

Lord and Savior, "Tell me, what have I done wrong? Show me my rebellion and my sin. Why do you turn away from me? Why do you consider me your enemy? Would you terrify a leaf that is blown by the wind? Would you chase a dry stalk of grass? You write bitter accusations against me and bring up all the sins of my youth." "But who can detect their errors? Clear me from hidden faults." Restore me again, O God, and cause Your face to shine in pleasure and approval on me, and I shall be saved! (Job 13:23-26 NLT; Ps. 19:12 NRSV not paraphrased; Ps. 80:3 AMP paraphrased)

Prayers, Praises, and Personal Notes

_____

_____

_____

Spiritual Turning Point

"There must be a spiritual renewal of your thoughts and attitudes. You must display a new nature because you are a new person, created in God's likeness—righteous, holy, and true."

EPHESIANS 4:23-24 NLT

*G*eri and Dave had worked side by side in the photography business and as missionaries during their entire thirty years of marriage. They were seldom apart from one another. Then Dave developed Alzheimer's disease. As her husband became increasingly incapacitated, Geri's role in life changed dramatically.

"I felt like my security blanket had been yanked from beneath me," she related. "I felt helpless, very fragile, and unable to make decisions without him. He had taken total care of me, made all the decisions (usually taking my opinion into account), and paid all the bills. I couldn't function without him and had a great fear of being left alone."

Due to imagined and real inadequacies, Geri didn't think she could continue to do the prayer ministry that was now hers alone. But she prayed a lot, and God began to send the help she needed. As Geri reached out to God and received His resources to deal with her situation, she came to a turning point in her struggles.

Personal Identity Crises

Major life changes such as Geri experienced can cause an identity crisis. "Our sense of personal identity depends largely on the roles we play and the relationships we have. What we do and who we know contributes significantly to how we understand ourselves. Catastrophic loss is like undergoing an amputation of a limb."[1]

Some people have an identity crisis when they go through a divorce or serious illness, lose a job or a loved one, or experience any other life-changing loss. They are no longer defined by a role that gave them significance and around which their life centered. They lose their sense of belonging or no longer feel needed when their personal relationships and responsibilities dramatically change. They're not sure who they are, what to do, or how to function because the person or position that gave them purpose is gone.

Until people lose a loved one, they don't realize how much that person defined their life or gave them a sense of security. They had someone they lived for and loved; now they feel confused, empty, and lost without him or her. People who have lost a spouse often say: "I feel like half a person."

Gerald Sittser wrote about his identity crisis from being widowed: "What defines me as a person—my sexuality, my intellect, my feelings, my convictions, my plans—still searches for her [his wife] like a homing pigeon for its roost. But the self I once was cannot find its old place to land. It is homeless now."[2]

In an identity crisis, a person may shut down emotionally and physically, make irrational or wrong choices, or choose a self-destructive lifestyle. Who one is as a person will be affected in a positive or negative way depending on how he or she copes with changing roles and relationships. "This crisis of identity, however, can lead to the formation of a new identity that integrates the loss into it."[3]

Faith Crises

In the spiritual reaction phase, we can experience both an identity and a faith crisis. This can be a decisive moment when we turn away from our faith or draw closer to the Lord. A series of losses, trials, and/or disappointments can bring us to this culminating point.

Clare shared about her crisis of faith. "I'd been struggling and wanted to leave our church, but the people were such a loving family. The minister, however, preached condemning messages and was often sarcastic to the people.

"When a dearly loved young man was killed in an accident, the minister used the funeral service as a platform to chastise and condemn the youth. The loss of a friend was heartbreaking enough, but his "message" hurt people even more. For many years afterward I struggled with my faith and wondered that God would allow this man to hurt so many people. I joined a different church, but many young people were so hurt that they left that funeral service and never attended church again."

Here are some examples of other painful experiences that can cause Christians to have a crisis of faith: Church members or leaders are divisive, have theological disputes, or fight among themselves. A church splits, relationships are severed, and people are wounded or fall away spiritually. Some Christians' bitter, judgmental, rigid, or unforgiving attitudes hurt others in their faith. Cliques, coldness, and exclusion of certain people cause deep spiritual wounds.

People lose faith due to the fall of other Christians, especially those in leadership. Others commit a wrong and refuse to be restored with the Lord and those whom they hurt. People's faith can fail when they burn out due to over-involvement in church activities and ministries.

Personal trials can cause a crisis of faith. Adversity continues over a prolonged period with little relief, or a person is devastated by a series of losses. Christians feel God has failed them because He doesn't answer prayer as they had hoped. They doubt His love for them. They feel abandoned by a pastor or church members in a time of need. Other Christians make insensitive or judgmental remarks about someone's loss or affliction.

Being a Christian for more than forty-three years has convinced me that no one would have a committed relationship with the Lord if one's faith were based on hurt feelings, trials, or how we Christians wound one another. If we're going to keep on our pilgrimage of faith, we need to work through our grief and pain, forgive those who wounded us or seek their forgiveness, and become a more compassionate Christlike person toward others.

Accepting Loss

Accepting our trials and losses means that we have a more hopeful attitude and a desire to grow and learn from them. We remember them without bitterness or dwelling on them. We accept our change in identity and are willing to take on new roles and responsibilities. Acceptance frees us to let go, move forward, and open ourselves to a different kind of life.

Tim Hansel was injured in an accident and has suffered severe pain ever since. He wrote in *You Gotta Keep Dancin'*, "Some people spend their entire life waiting for that which will never, and can never, happen. Limitations are not necessarily negative. In fact, I'm beginning to believe that they can give life definition, clarity, and *freedom*. We are called to a freedom *of* and *in* limitations—not *from*."[4]

We need to accept and be grateful for the freedom we have even in our limitations. "Despite our inability to control circumstances, we are given the gift of being free to respond to our situation in our own way, creatively or destructively."[5] Acceptance means we look for positive, creative ways to live within our limitations.

Spiritually Accepting Loss

Tim Hansel describes some of the steps people must take to come through a faith crisis. "Pain forces you to look below the surface. The tragedy is that many of us never have the courage to choose to do that. Hence we waste much of our life in bitterness and complaint, always looking for something else, never realizing that perhaps God has already given us sufficient grace to discover all of what we are looking for in the midst of our circumstances."

As we begin to accept the changes in our lives brought about by losses, we move out of the spiritual reaction phase into the spiritual rebuilding phase. We desire to grow spiritually within the limits of our present situation rather than waiting for the Lord to change it or provide something better.

Hansel explains, "Acceptance means that I accept the process. It has been said that Jesus came not to take away suffering, but to help us make our suffering more like his and to give it meaning." We become more like Christ by taking up our cross and following Him.

"Acceptance means that I allow the process to transform me into the image of God's Son. It means that I'm willing to let go of who I think I ought to be and become who God wants me to be."[6] I'm willing to let God work in my life just as I am—not as I think I should be. I humbly accept what He desires to do in and through me in my present condition.

Another writer, Gerald Sittser, points out that "we can learn simply to be, whether we are divorced, unemployed, widowed, abused, sick, or even dying. We can allow ourselves to be loved as creatures made in God's image, though our bodies are broken, our thoughts confused, and our emotions troubled. And we can start to become hopeful that life can still be good, although never in the way it was before."[7]

Turning Points

We come to a turning point as we accept our losses and the changes in our identity, roles, and responsibilities. We determine that we won't become stuck in past pain, but we'll get on with our life. Here are some signs that we've made that turn: We realize that we're no longer obsessed by a painful experience; it doesn't dominate our thinking. We go for longer periods of time without feelings of sadness. We aren't dwelling on the past and longing for what used to be or will never happen.

We no longer harbor bitter, harmful attitudes. We've begun adapting, gaining a new sense of belonging, and settling into a routine. We have more energy and are doing more of our normal tasks. We're trying new activities and making friends.

In *Surviving Grief . . . and Learning to Live Again*, Catherine Sanders explains what may bring about these changes: "Sometimes an external event makes a difference in turning our grief around—a vacation gives us a new perspective, a new job moves us from one environment to another, or a return to school takes us into a completely different atmosphere. Anything that lifts us out of our rut and places us in a different routine, or around new people, can make a difference in how we perceive the world."[8]

According to Elizabeth Harper Neeld, signs of a turning point also include "a series of realizations, understandings, actions, and commitments. . . . We shift our focus. We experience a change in perspective." We have a more hopeful outlook and see the possibility of new opportunities. "We can now imagine our lives extending out into the future, something that didn't seem possible, or even likely, earlier in our grieving."[9]

As we change and grow through loss, we have a renewed sense of identity. Hopefully, we become less self-centered and more caring, less critical of other hurting people and more kind and understanding. Even our values, priorities, and perspective on life changes.

We appreciate loved ones more and small daily blessings. We treasure what we do have, the time we've been given, and the things we can do. "Coming full circle is what grieving is about: to come to terms with the loss and to arrive at a point where you go back to your way of living and seeing life as worthwhile."[10]

Spiritual Turning Points

When we're in the spiritual reaction phase, we often have to come to the end of ourselves before we realize we can't go on the way we are. "But in coming to the end of ourselves, we can also come to the beginning of a vital relationship with God. Our failures can lead us to grace and to a profound spiritual awakening," writes Gerald Sittser in *A Grace Disguised*.

When we are awakened to this realization, we are at a turning point and ready for the Lord to rebuild our lives spiritually. As Sittser says, "In coming to the end of ourselves, we have come to the beginning of our true and deepest selves. We have found the One whose love gives shape to our being."[11]

We know we have reached a spiritual turning point when we realize that our identity is found in Christ, not in other people, circumstances, or our position in life. We are more aware of God's ever-loving presence and working in our lives. We have a fresh desire for God's Word and long to know His will and seek His guidance. We know we have changed directions when we have a richer prayer life, recognize how the Lord is changing us, and are growing in faith. We're more committed to being faithful in worshiping the Lord and serving Him in our church and other ministries.

Letting Go and Changing Our Attitude

Coming to a personal and spiritual turning point and making changes also includes letting go and moving on with our life. We need to give up attitudes and behaviors that keep us trapped in grief. This step frees us to "create new ways of thinking and behaving that are useful—that will allow us to create a satisfying life for the future."[12]

The process necessary for creating a satisfactory life includes accepting losses, turning toward what today holds, making positive changes, and letting go. Letting go means we accept our situation the way it is and move on with our life.

Letting go means that we stop trying to control others and solve everyone's problems. We throw away the "history book" of past offenses and become a more forgiving person. We stop criticizing and judging others but search out our own shortcomings and correct them. Letting go means changing our attitude even when we can't change anything else about our life.

Dr. Victor Frankl maintains that one's attitude is the one freedom that can't be taken from him or her—even in the darkest pit of a World War II prison camp. "We who lived in concentration camps can remember the men who walked through the huts comforting others, giving away their last piece of bread. They may have been few in number, but they offer sufficient proof that everything can be taken from a man but one thing: the last of human freedoms—to choose one's attitude in any given set of circumstances. . . ."[13]

Geri, whose story opened this chapter, shared how having an accepting attitude helped her when her husband became ill. "I read an article about research conducted at Harvard University, which indicated that attitude is far more important than intelligence, education, or special talent. The study concluded that up to 85 percent of success in life is due to attitude, while the other 15 percent is due to our ability. If my attitude was that important, I wanted to be an encourager.

"Many have asked how I coped with the living death of my husband. I'll have to say that prayer and my attitude, along with educating myself about the disease were the best coping skills I had. I wrote in a diary before retiring each evening, recording the positive things that had happened that day.

Looking for blessings and remembering them helped tremendously. After Dave went to the nursing home, I journaled what I did that day that was a blessing—things I couldn't have done had Dave still been with me.

"Our last three anniversaries were celebrated at his nursing home. I could have been hurt that he hadn't said my name in nearly two years. Instead I focused on his huge smile and the twinkle in his eyes that spoke volumes of love. That told me I was someone important to him.

"Now that Dave is gone, I often read our life verses, Philippians 4:4-9: 'Whatsoever things are of good report . . . think on these things.' Looking back, I remember the fun times we often had together in our thirty-eight years of marriage. Looking forward, I remind myself that a grateful, positive attitude will help me continue to be an encouragement to others."

Letting Go Spiritually

Now we are ready to move onto the spiritual renewal phase. We put on our new identity in Christ by continually renewing the attitude and spirit of our mind. We put on the new self created in the likeness of God to be holy, righteous, and true (Eph. 4:23-24).

Moreover, letting go spiritually means that we admit we are powerless and that the outcome is not in our hands but in God's. We fear less and trust the Lord more. We don't allow past hurts and our own failures to cripple our faith. We humbly rely on the Lord to renew us, restore us, and enable us to be and do what He desires. We offer Him sacrifices of praise and thanksgiving. Letting go means letting God be in control—for He is.

LETTING GO OF YESTERDAY

My burdens today are from yesterday, but the past I cannot change.
No matter what I do there's not a thing I can rearrange.
The burdens on my heart are so heavy that I carry from yesterday.
What could I have done differently, and would it change today?
The 'if onlys' and 'what ifs' are not for me to know.
For God leads me step by step, and He is in control.
I need to look to the future and let go of the past.
Although at times it's difficult, to God I will hold fast.
I'll trust in Him and realize that He's taking care of me.
I'll let go of yesterday's burdens, and from them I'll be set free.[14]

Scripture Reading: Job 19:13-22

Practicing the Spiritual Life

How did others treat Job, causing him to have a kind of identity crisis?

_____

_____

If you ever experienced a personal identity crisis due to painful changes, explain what happened, how others treated you, and what you felt.

_____

_____

In what ways do you desire to grow spiritually through such a crisis?

_____

_____

Prayer

Ever-caring Lord, "I am scorned by all my enemies and despised by my neighbors—even my friends are afraid to come near me. When they see me on the street, they turn the other way. I have been ignored as if I were dead, as if I were a broken pot." "But I am trusting you, O Lord, saying, 'You are my God!'" "Return, O Lord, and rescue me. Save me because of your unfailing love." "Lord, don't hold back your tender mercies from me. My only hope is in your unfailing love and faithfulness." (Ps. 31:11-12, 14 NLT; Ps. 6:4 NLT; Ps. 40:11 NLT not paraphrased)

Prayers, Praises, and Personal Notes

_____

_____

_____

Scripture Reading: Job 2:8-9

Practicing the Spiritual Life

Job's wife had a spiritual crisis after she lost her ten children and her husband became ill with painful boils. What was her spiritual reaction?

_____

_____

_____

If you've had a crisis of faith, what caused it? What did you say and feel?

_____

_____

_____

Prayer

O Lord, the "tongue is a small thing, but what enormous damage it can do. A tiny spark can set a great forest on fire. And the tongue is a flame of fire. It is full of wickedness that can ruin your whole life. It can turn the entire course of your life into a blazing flame of destruction." "Sometimes it praises our Lord and Father, and sometimes it breaks out into curses against those who have been made in the image of God. And so blessing and cursing come pouring out of the same mouth." But "gentle words bring life and health." "Kind words are like honey—sweet to the soul and healthy for the body." Therefore, "I said to myself, 'I will watch what I do and not sin in what I say. I will curb my tongue.'" (James 3:5-6a, 9-10a NLT; Prov. 15:4a NLT; Prov. 16:24 NLT; Ps. 39:1a NLT not paraphrased)

Prayers, Praises, and Personal Notes

_____

_____

_____

Scripture Reading: Luke 22:31-34, 55-62

Practicing the Spiritual Life

When Peter failed, he had a crisis of faith. How did he react?

_____

_____

Describe any time when you alternated between trusting God and turning away from Him during a trial.

_____

_____

How will you strengthen your faith so it won't fail when you go through testing?

_____

_____

Prayer

Hear my prayer, O Lord, and give ear to my weeping; do not hold Your peace at my tears. For I will examine myself, making sure my faith is genuine, proving and testing my own self. I won't profess that I know You and then in words and actions deny You. Lord, I ask You now to increase my faith. (Ps. 39:12a KJV; 2 Cor. 13:5a KJV; Titus 1:16a KJV; Luke 17:5 KJV, all paraphrased)

Prayers, Praises, and Personal Notes

_____

_____

_____

_____

Scripture Reading: John 21:14-17

Practicing the Spiritual Life

After Peter's crisis of faith, what did Jesus ask him and then tell him to do?

_____

_____

_____

This was a spiritual turning point for Peter that helped him let go of his failure and find spiritual renewal. About what hurts or failures do you need to do the same?

_____

_____

_____

Prayer

O my Shepherd, I am Yours, a sheep of Your flock. I will thank You always; forever and ever I will praise You. "I love you, O Lord, my strength." I love You, Lord my God, with all my heart and with all my soul and with all my mind and with all my strength. And I will love my neighbor as myself. There are no commandments greater than these to love God and man. (Ps. 79:13 NCV paraphrased; Ps. 18:1 not paraphrased; Mark 12:30-31 paraphrased)

Prayers, Praises, and Personal Notes

_____

_____

_____

_____

_____

Scripture Reading: Romans 14:1-13

Practicing the Spiritual Life

What causes Christians to be weakened in their faith?

_____

_____

What actions of ours can cause other Christians to have a crisis of faith?

_____

_____

In what ways did this passage speak to you about your faith and/or your attitude and actions toward other Christians?

_____

_____

Prayer

Spirit of God, I'll keep watching and praying that I may not enter into temptation; my spirit is willing, but my flesh is weak. I will take care that this liberty of mine does not somehow become a stumbling block to the weak. For if I sin against members of my family and wound their conscience when it is weak, I sin against You, Christ. To the weak I will become weak so that I might win the weak. I will become all things to all people so that I might by all means save some. (Matt. 26:41 NAS95; 1 Cor. 8:9, 12 NRSV; 1 Cor. 9:22 NRSV, all paraphrased)

Prayers, Praises, and Personal Notes

_____

_____

_____

Scripture Reading: Romans 14:14-23; 15:1-2

Practicing the Spiritual Life

How do we please the Lord and build up others in their faith?

_____

_____

_____

This week what will you do specifically to build up and spiritually encourage another Christian?

_____

_____

_____

Prayer

Yes, Lord, I will continue to build my life on the foundation of my holy faith and continue to pray as I am directed by the Holy Spirit. I'll show mercy to those whose faith is wavering. I will encourage others and build them up. I'll show by my good life that my works are done with gentleness born of wisdom. And now all glory to You, Lord, who are able to keep me from stumbling, and who will bring me into Your glorious presence innocent of sin and with great joy. (Jude 1:20, 22 NLT; 1 Thess. 5:11a; James 3:13b NRSV; Jude 1:24 NLT, all paraphrased)

Prayers, Praises, and Personal Notes

_____

_____

_____

_____

Scripture Reading: Ephesians 4:22-24

Practicing the Spiritual Life

How are we spiritually renewed?

Note the ways you have been made new in the attitudes of your mind, have put on the new self, and have grown spiritually.

Prayer

Jesus, I will not lie to others since I have taken off my old self with its prac-tices. In its place I will clothe myself with a brand-new nature that is contin-ually being renewed as I learn more and more about You, Christ, who created this new nature within me. For, Holy Spirit, when You control my life, You will produce this kind of fruit in me—love, joy, peace, patience, kindness, goodness, faithfulness, gentleness, and self-control. Since I belong to You, Christ Jesus, I will nail the passions and desires of my sinful nature to Your cross and crucify them there. I am living now by Your power, Holy Spirit, and I will follow Your leading in every part of my life. (Col. 3:9; Col. 3:10 NLT; Gal. 5:22, 23a-25 NLT, all paraphrased)

Prayers, Praises, and Personal Notes

Search for Spiritual Meaning

"Can anything ever separate us from Christ's love?
Does it mean he no longer loves us
if we have trouble or calamity,
or are persecuted, or are hungry or cold
or in danger or threatened with death?"
"No, despite all these things, overwhelming victory
is ours through Christ, who loved us."

ROMANS 8:35, 37 NLT

*E*ight-year-old Mike had just been awarded his Cub Scout Wolf badge. This pleased his parents, Bob and Shirlee, but there were other things about Mike that made him special. His sensitivity toward others, such as the money Mike earned or that he received on his birthdays was put aside and usually spent on others. He brought home holiday treats from school to share with his younger sister and two brothers. It was a familiar sight to see Mike kneeling beside them, helping them fix a toy or patiently explaining how a game was played.

But Mike had been experiencing acute pain in his back, and Bob and Shirlee took him to the hospital for a week of tests. Shirlee tells the story of what happened.

"It was Good Friday. My husband, Bob, was with Mike at the hospital. Bob called me and wanted me to come right away, but I pressed him to tell me the results. After a long pause, he said, 'Honey, it's leukemia.'

"Bob had prepared himself for the reality of Mike's death. I hadn't. I held onto the hope that a miracle could save him. There was none. He died a year after he was diagnosed with cancer, leaving behind forever the hopes and dreams a mother has for her firstborn.

"'It's part of God's plan.' 'He has a purpose in this.' We heard those words again and again from consoling friends and clergy. I searched frantically to uncover a purpose. *It had better be something big,* I thought. *My son gave his life for it—whatever it is.*

"For a while I thought that writing about Mike might give his life meaning. I wrote and submitted his story to a magazine, but it was rejected. I, too, felt rejected. Then Bob and I considered adopting a handicapped child, but when we decided we couldn't do that, I felt another door had closed.

"'God, what is Your purpose?' I cried.

"Looking back thirty-three years later, I remember how important it was for me to find a purpose for Mike's early death. My search was a frenzied one. Now I know that God loved Mike and loves me, too. It's no longer important for me to know why he died. God's love surpasses anything I could envision. I've learned to trust Him completely, to trust in His timing, His wisdom. I believe that everything in my life has happened because He allowed it for a purpose even when I don't know what it might be."

The Mystery of Suffering

Our faith is challenged by the mystery of suffering, its purpose, and God's part in it all. We know that "God is love" (1 John 4:8b), but how can we say that as we look upon the ravages of abuse, atrocities, famine, the Holocaust, murder, natural disasters, poverty, prejudice, war, and all kinds of cruelty and vile evil?

If God loves us, why is there so much suffering and evil in this world? Why do bad things happen to innocent children and good people? Where is God in suffering? What good can possibly come from affliction?

Is God punishing us for our sins? How come we have to go through the same kinds of trials over and over again? What lessons are we supposed to be learning? Why do we keep missing the point God's trying to make—whatever it is? If only we could figure it out, then maybe we wouldn't suffer anymore.

Job questioned the unfairness and mystery of suffering. "Why do the wicked live on, growing old and increasing in power?" (Job 21:7). "One dies in full prosperity, being wholly at ease and secure." "Another dies in bitterness of soul, never having tasted of good" (Job 21:23, 25 NRSV).

Questions asked about the whys of suffering are endless. Throughout the ages volumes have been written in an attempt to answer them. Though we debate the reasons God allows worldwide suffering, *most often we are concerned about the seemingly senseless losses that devastate our lives and loved ones.*

If you're in the midst of a hard trial, you want God to answer your prayers and relieve you of your heartache. If He doesn't answer, then you want to understand why. And if the solution to your trial is relatively simple but beyond your reach, then it seems even more senseless.

Edith Schaeffer wrote, "I believe that wherever God can point out to Satan one child of His being stoned and dying with unbroken love for Him, He can point out another being stoned with as many stones and yet being protected from dying in answer to prayer."[1] But why should one die and the other live? That, too, is a mystery.

"The hardest ingredient in suffering is often *time.* A short, sharp pang is easily borne, but when a sorrow drags its weary way through long, monotonous years, and day after day returns with the same dull routine of hopeless agony, the heart loses its strength and, without the grace of God, is sure to sink into the very sullenness of despair."[2]

Why does suffering go on so long for some people while others are quickly relieved of their trials? Why is one person healed of cancer while another one suffers for years with the same kind of cancer? We simply do not know.

Though the following statements will not comfort us, they are truths with which we must come to terms: God allows us to suffer because we bear the consequences of living in a sinful world. Satan's evil works, natural disasters, our diseased condition, and human sin are the major causes of trials.

We inherited this conflict between good and evil; it was our condition at birth. Moreover, God doesn't violate our free will. We are free to do good or evil. Free will is our greatest blessing and greatest curse. We all bear the curse of sin and affliction.

One of the first explanations given for suffering is: "They must have sinned." That may well be true. But why do some suffer greatly for a seemingly "minor" sin while others who commit terrible crimes escape justice or hardly suffer at all?

Some other reasons people offer for suffering are: "God can trust him or her with more suffering." "It is all a part of God's plan." "She was in so much pain and such a special person that God wanted her to be with Him."

It's easy to give those kinds of answers until you're grieving a heartbreaking loss, and then they provide no comfort at all. They only give rise to more questions. "Does it mean that God doesn't trust me if I don't suffer much?" "Since God is without sin, how can His plans be evil and harmful?" "Does it mean that I'm not special to God if I live on in unbearable pain when I want to die and be with Him?"

We can get caught in a never-ending cycle of questions and rebuttals. We will never find answers that satisfy us because in our human reasoning suffering doesn't make sense. We don't know why we or others experience a specific trial or loss or why some suffer more and others less—outside of the fact that we live in a fallen world.

"The awful problem of suffering continually crops up in the Scriptures and in life and remains a mystery. From Job until now, and from before Job, the mystery of suffering remains," states Oswald Chambers.[3] The heart of this mystery is that no matter how much we want to know the reasons for affliction, we won't be satisfied until the Lord relieves us or a loved one of suffering.

Therefore, it shouldn't surprise us when people conclude that God is distant, silent, indifferent, and impersonal. He didn't answer or come to their rescue the way they expected, and they're disillusioned and disappointed. Phil Yancey addresses this attitude. "If we insist on visible proofs from God, we may well prepare the way for a permanent state of disappointment. True faith does not so much attempt to manipulate God to do our will as it does to position us to do his will."[4]

Gerald Sittser had prayed for years for his family's safety, and every night he thanked the Lord for answering. After an auto accident that took his mother, wife, and daughter, he was hesitant about praying for anything. He said, "I was tortured by the question of where God was that night. I wondered whether I could ever again be able to trust him. I longed to continue believing in God. It was bad enough to lose three members of my family. Why make things worse by losing God, too? I realized that he was the only foundation on which to build my broken life."[5]

The alternative to not having the Lord as our spiritual foundation in affliction is to have no foundation at all. What is worse—suffering with God or without Him? Without Him we have no hope and nothing to look forward to. The only one we can count on for His constant presence and support is God. Heaven awaits us, and when we reach there, understanding why we suffered will not be important at all.

We have to come to the point of accepting that God is sovereign, which means He has supreme and unlimited power over everyone and everything. Yet He allows for our free will and Satan's evil. What a mystery!

Gerald Sittser explains, "God's sovereignty, then, transcends human freedom but does not nullify it. Both are real—only real in different ways and on different planes. Belief in God's sovereignty thus gives us the security of knowing God is in control, but it also assigns us the responsibility of using our freedom to make wise choices and to remain faithful to him."

Unless we can come to terms with God and the mystery of suffering, we will blame Him, complain against Him, and even turn away from our faith. "Suffering may push us far enough in the direction of doubt that we arrive at atheism," warns Sittser.[6] *If we're going to continue on our pilgrimage of faith, we need to change our focus from trying to understand why we suffer to finding meaning in affliction and realizing God's comforting presence.*

Searching for and Discovering Personal Meaning

"One of the greatest tragedies of our modern civilization is that you and I can live a trivial life and get away with it. One of the great advantages of pain and suffering is that it forces us to break through our superficial crusts to discover life on a deeper and more meaningful level."[7]

Suffering forces us to look below the surface. It plunges us into the depths and strips us of shallow concerns. But will we accept the challenge to suffer with courage and grace and to discover the meaning it has for our lives and for others as well?

If we accept this challenge, we must also realize that "life has a meaning up to the last moment, and it retains this meaning literally to the end. In other words, life's meaning is an unconditional one, for it even includes the potential meaning of suffering"[8] when we or a loved one may be dying.

We must realize that "if there is a meaning in life at all, then there must be a meaning in suffering. . . . Without suffering and death human life cannot be complete."[9] Even in the worst afflictions, we can find meaning in the treasured moments of our life.

Morrie Schwartz was dying of a degenerative disease when he wrote, "I have multiple goals to help give my life meaning. Dealing warmly and closely and lovingly with my friends and family is a top priority. There are plenty of books I plan to read. I have my favorite pieces of music I look forward to hearing."[10]

In your own search for meaning in suffering, you need to find out how it has changed you as a person. You can discover this by writing down how trials have affected your life both for the good and bad. The purpose for this is to help you gain some objectivity and understand where you are in the healing process. Affirm the positive changes that you are making rather than dwelling on your failures. Finally, make goals that take into account your losses and limitations and that can help you find purpose.

Doing a special project can help us find meaning. For example, if a loved one has died, "we may find the greatest peace by exploring what our beloved person's life has meant. Sometimes it is helpful to put together a photo album of all our pictures of the person or a scrapbook of mementos. By doing this, we are able to see the chronology of events and get a more compete view of the person's life."[11]

Searching for and Discovering Spiritual Meaning

In the spiritual rebuilding phase, our quest for meaning in affliction is an essential part of the healing process. The purpose we desire to find, however, is often far different than God's.

Moreover, as Dr. Victor Frankl maintains, the search for spiritual "meaning is unique and specific in that it must and can be fulfilled" by each person alone. No one else can relieve us of our grief and inner pain or suffer in our place. "What matters, therefore, is not the meaning of life in general but rather the specific meaning of a person's life at a given moment."[12]

God has one plan of salvation through Christ, but what He desires to achieve through suffering in each Christian's life is different. Our unique opportunity is the way we bear affliction and loss and refute Satan's lies that our faith will fail. Finding spiritual meaning is different for each one of us. It constantly changes, depending upon the trials we're experiencing and our opportunities to glorify the Lord in suffering.

We need to accept trials as our spiritual task, as our opportunity to grow and demonstrate genuine faith. Suffering is not only our spiritual task, but it is part of God's work in us—the greatest work He may ever accomplish in and through us. Moreover, the building up of our spiritual courage and faith during heartaches gives them meaning.

Though our life may not be what we want it to be or what we planned, we can discover a deeper level of appreciation for what we do have even in our sorrow. We realize that it is possible to "live in and be enlarged by loss"[13] as we discover a whole new dimension of faith.

How is our faith enlarged by loss? *First, we need to realize that God is present with us and helps us in all our suffering.* We need to accept comforting support from the Lord, who is constantly beside us in our darkest hours. Our Comforter is always within us tenderly caring for our broken hearts.

But if all we think about is what God is not doing for us, our grief is intensified and our faith weakened. If we keep looking for outward evidences that God is working, change is coming about, or how soon our suffering will be relieved, we'll be disappointed every time. As we dwell on thoughts that God is always with us and supporting us, we're more aware and appreciative of His tender care.

Jesus promised, "Never will I leave you; never will I forsake you" (Heb. 13:5b). "And surely I am with you always, to the very end of the age" (Matt. 28:20) We need to keep our minds and hearts on the Lord Himself and affirm His loving presence and support in suffering.

Second, our afflictions last a microsecond in comparison to living forevermore in heaven, where we'll be free from all suffering. "Even if we have an affliction or time of brokenness that lasts for years, even decades, what is that compared to all of eternity?"[14] "For this slight momentary affliction is preparing us for an eternal weight of glory beyond all measure" (2 Cor. 4:17 NRSV).

Third, our spiritual life is deepened through suffering. Dr. Victor Frankl wrote about the richness of spiritual life among some of his fellow prisoners of war: "In spite of all the enforced physical and mental primitiveness of the life in a concentration camp, it was possible for spiritual life to deepen. . . . They [inmates] were able to retreat from their terrible surroundings to a life of inner riches and spiritual freedom."[15]

Gerald Sittser also said, "The Incarnation means that God cares so much that he chose to become human and suffer loss, though he never had to. I have grieved long and hard and intensely. But I have found comfort knowing that the sovereign God, who is in control of everything, is the same God who has experienced the pain I live with every day. No matter how deep the pit into which I descend, I keep finding God there."[16]

We may be stripped of our dignity and everything precious to us, and suffer terrible deprivation, even torture. But no human, no evil force can deprive us of God's presence. No one can take away our spiritual freedom in our innermost thought life. We are free to pray, fix our minds on Christ, meditate on His Word, and worship Him in hymn and song. Even if our Bibles were taken from us, the Holy Spirit would bring verses and hymns to mind to comfort and strengthen us.

God Is with Us and Loves Us

One of our greatest fears is that we suffer for no reason, and that if we are incapacitated, we will have no value to others. Our society has devalued life and in doing so has devalued suffering. To most people pain is pointless and has no meaning other than being an inconvenience that must be done away with.

The truth we must hold on to is that the sacrifices we make in affliction and the way we trust the Lord have great significance in His eyes. No matter how crippled or seriously ill we or a loved one becomes, God values and loves us. His love for us is not based on our condition. His love is absolutely unconditional.

In Romans 8:31-39, we have God's assurance of His ever-faithful love in suffering. "What can we say about such wonderful things as these? If God is for us, who can ever be against us?" (Rom. 8:31 NLT).

"*God is for us.* He, as our Judge, is satisfied; as our Father, he loves us; as the supreme and almighty Controller of events, who works all things after the counsel of his own will, he has determined to save us; and as that Being whose love is as unchanging as it is infinite, he allows nothing to separate his children from himself."[17]

"Since God did not spare even his own Son but gave him up for us all, won't God, who gave us Christ, also give us everything else?" (Rom. 8:32 NLT). What we need to realize most of all is the depth of God's love for us in our suffering. We need to receive the Lord's passionate, unfailing, ever-forgiving love. "I have loved you with an everlasting love; I have drawn you with loving-kindness" (Jer. 31:3).

That is the very foundation of God's love and our faith, but do we believe it with all our hearts, not just with our minds? You are so valuable to God that He gave His one and only Son Jesus to die for *you.* "The cross of Jesus is the supreme evidence of the love of God."[18] "This is love: not that we loved God, but that he loved us and sent his Son as an atoning sacrifice for our sins" (1 John 4:10). The miracle of God's love is that it is everlasting and limitless, a free gift that cannot be earned.

"Can anything ever separate us from Christ's love? Does it mean he no longer loves us if we have trouble or calamity, or are persecuted, or are hungry or cold or in danger or threatened with death?" (Rom. 8:35 NLT). Isn't this truth the opposite of what we usually think? If God loves us He wouldn't allow us to go through all these things.

Those trials do not change our position with God in Christ Jesus. It is because of the reign of sin that we suffer. He allows us to be disciplined by trials to spiritually refine us, but that does not change God's relationship with us. We are eternally secure in His love through Christ Jesus.

Deprivation and hardships can and do affect the closeness of our relationship with the Lord. It is only natural to feel abandoned and separated from Him when we suffer trials. "But none of them is able to come between the love of God and the soul of a saint on the spiritual level."[19]

"A true Christian loves Christ never the less though he suffer for him, thinks never the worse of Christ though he lose all for him."[20] Though hardships and trials may weaken us emotionally and physically, they actually benefit us spiritually. As we continue to hold on to our faith and love the Lord, we not only ward off Satan's accusations against us, but the glory of Christ's victory is increased in us.

"(Even the Scriptures say, 'For your sake we are killed every day; we are being slaughtered like sheep.') No, despite all these things, overwhelming victory is ours through Christ, who loved us" (Rom. 8:36-37 NLT). Jesus promised, "My sheep listen to my voice; I know them . . . and they shall never perish; no one can snatch them out of my hand" (John 10:27a-28b).

Shepherds must constantly protect their sheep from predators. Christ has given us the spiritual assurance that "none of his sheep will perish, not one. . . . The Shepherd is so careful of their welfare that he has them not only within his fold, but *in his hand,* and taken under his special protection. Yet their enemies are so daring that they attempt to pluck them out of his hand; but they cannot, they shall not do it."[21]

Absolutely nothing can separate us from God's love. "That is, whatever we may be called on to suffer in this life, nothing can deprive us of the love of him who died for us and who now lives to plead our cause in heaven."[22]

We can say with complete assurance, "The Lord is on my side to help me" (Ps. 118:7a NRSV). He shields, sustains, and supports me (Ps. 18:2; 54:4; 94:18). "God is our refuge and strength, an ever-present help in trouble" (Ps. 46:1).

"In the future, when trials and difficulties await you, do not be fearful. Let not this faith slip from you—God is love; whisper it not only to your heart in its hour of darkness, but here in your corner of God's earth. Live in the belief of it . . . sing it in consecrated moments of peaceful joy."[23]

"Whatever your circumstance is right now, and whatever mine is, we have the immediate opportunity for defeating Satan and bringing glory to God. How? First, by whispering to Him, 'I love You and trust You,' and asking that He increase that trust and love. Second, by longing for an increase of truth within us as we say, 'Not my will but Thine be done.'"[24]

Keep surrendering yourself to God that He may accomplish His will and purposes in your life and through your suffering. Keep your commitment to Christ and defeat Satan's accusations that your faith and love for the Lord will fail. "Keep yourselves in God's love as you wait for the mercy of our Lord Jesus Christ to bring you to eternal life" (Jude 21).

Practice keeping yourself in His loving presence. Fix your thoughts on the Lord, His provisions, and the simple everyday kindnesses that come to you. "Jesus loves me." Shout it if you must! "Jesus loves me!" Repeat it again and again, refusing to entertain any doubts. "Do not live at a distance from God; live near Him, delighting yourself in Him. Remove all barriers of selfishness and fear and plunge into the fathomless love of God."[25]

JESUS LOVES ME

Jesus loves me when my way is rough and steep.
He comforts me when my heart is broken and I weep.
Jesus loves me when problems overwhelm my soul.
He holds me close when life's difficulties take their toll.
Jesus loves me when grief and loss are heavy on my heart.
He gives me strength when my world is falling apart.
Jesus loves me when I'm hurting and nothing seems right.
He cares for me when I worry and can't sleep at night.
Jesus loves me, and from my heartaches I'll be free,
When He takes me home to heaven for all eternity.[26]

Scripture Reading: Deuteronomy 31:1-8

Practicing the Spiritual Life

We need to accept trials as our spiritual task, as our opportunity to grow and demonstrate genuine faith. With what attitude were the Israelites to face the frightening prospect of taking possession of the land?

_____

_____

What did Moses twice promise the people the Lord would do for them?

_____

_____

About what difficult and frightening trials do you need the assurance that the Lord will never forsake you?

_____

_____

Prayer

Almighty Protector, You have commanded me: "Be strong and courageous; do not be frightened or dismayed, for the Lord your God is with you wherever you go." "So we can say with confidence, 'The Lord is my helper; I will not be afraid. What can anyone do to me?'" And, Jesus, I will remember, You are with me always, to the end of the age. (Josh. 1:9b NRSV; Heb. 13:6 NRSV not paraphrased; Matt. 28:20b NRSV paraphrased)

Prayers, Praises, and Personal Notes

_____

_____

_____

Scripture Reading: 2 Corinthians 4:13-16

Practicing the Spiritual Life

Why shouldn't we lose heart in suffering?

_____

_____

_____

In what ways have you moved from the spiritual reaction and rebuilding phases into spiritual renewal?

_____

_____

_____

Prayer

O God my Savior, when Your kindness and love appeared, You saved me, not because of righteous things I had done, but because of Your mercy. You saved me through the washing of rebirth and renewal by the Holy Spirit, whom You poured out on me generously through Jesus Christ my Savior. I have begun to live the new life, in which I am being made new and am becoming like the one who made me. This new life brings me the true knowledge of You, O God. For my hope is in You, Lord, who will renew my strength. (Titus 3:4-6; Col. 3:10 NCV; Isa. 40:31a, all paraphrased)

Prayers, Praises, and Personal Notes

_____

_____

_____

_____

Scripture Reading: 2 Corinthians 4:17-18

Practicing the Spiritual Life

How do our troubles compare to eternal glory?

_____

_____

Why should we fix our eyes on the unseen and not on our troubles?

_____

_____

In what ways do you desire to glorify Christ in your trials?

_____

_____

Prayer

Now, Lord, You are the Spirit, and where the Spirit of the Lord is, there is freedom. And I, who with an unveiled face reflect Your glory, Lord, am being transformed into Your likeness with ever-increasing glory, which comes from You, Lord, who are the Spirit. For my citizenship is in heaven, from which I also eagerly wait for You, my Savior, Lord Jesus Christ, who will transform my lowly body that it may be conformed to Your glorious body, according to the working by which You are able even to subdue all things to Yourself. All glory to You, who alone are God my Savior, through Jesus Christ my Lord. Yes, glory, majesty, power, and authority belong to You in the beginning, now, and forevermore. Amen. (2 Cor. 3:17-18; Phil. 3:20-21 NKJV; Jude 25 NLT, all paraphrased)

Prayers, Praises, and Personal Notes

_____

_____

_____

Scripture Reading: 1 John 4:10; Romans 8:31-32

Practicing the Spiritual Life

If our faith is going to be renewed in suffering, we need to realize the extent of God's love for us. How great is God's love, and what did He freely and graciously do for us?

_____

_____

_____

How does the greatness of God's love for you encourage you in your faith?

_____

_____

_____

Prayer

O Love eternal, I have known and believed the love that You have for me. God, You are love, and I who abide in love abide in You, O God, and You in me. Love has been perfected in me in this: that I may have boldness in the day of judgment; because as You are, so am I in this world. Yes, Jesus, I love You because You first loved me. (1 John 4:16-17, 19 NKJV, all paraphrased)

Prayers, Praises, and Personal Notes

_____

_____

_____

_____

_____

_____

_____

Scripture Reading: Romans 8:35-39

Practicing the Spiritual Life

Who or what cannot separate us from Christ's love?

_____

_____

_____

For what trials do you need to rely on the promise that nothing can separate you from God's love?

_____

_____

_____

Prayer

O Lord, I pray that from Your glorious, unlimited resources You will give me mighty inner strength through Your Holy Spirit. And I pray that, Christ, You will be more and more at home in my heart as I trust in You. May my roots go down deep into the soil of Your marvelous love. And may I have the power to understand, as all God's people should, how wide, how long, how high, and how deep Your love really is. May I experience Your love, Christ, though it is so great I will never fully understand it. Then I will be filled with the fullness of life and power that comes from You. Now glory be to You, Lord! By Your mighty power at work within me, You are able to accomplish infinitely more than I would ever dare to ask or hope. (Eph. 3:16-20 NLT paraphrased)

Prayers, Praises, and Personal Notes

_____

_____

_____

Scripture Reading: John 10:27-30

What does Jesus twice promise to assure us of His protection?

_____

_____

_____

How do you find comfort that you are safe in Jesus' arms?

_____

_____

_____

Prayer

Jesus, You are the Good Shepherd. As such You lay down Your life for the sheep. "The hired hand is not the shepherd who owns the sheep. So when he sees the wolf coming, he abandons the sheep and runs away. Then the wolf attacks the flock and scatters it. The man runs away because he is a hired hand and cares nothing for the sheep." Jesus, my Good Shepherd, You know me, and I know You—just as the Father knows You and You know the Father— and You lay down Your life for me. (John 10:11 paraphrased; 10:12-13 not paraphrased; 10:14-15 paraphrased)

Prayers, Praises, and Personal Notes

_____

_____

_____

_____

_____

_____

Scripture Reading: Psalm 46

Practicing the Spiritual Life

What can we say with complete assurance about God in times of personal and worldwide troubles?

_____

_____

_____

For what trials do you need to rely on the Lord to be your refuge, strength, and ever-present help?

_____

_____

_____

Prayer

"When I said, 'My foot is slipping,' your love, O Lord, supported me. When anxiety was great within me, your consolation brought joy to my soul." For "The Lord is my rock, my fortress and my deliverer; my God is my rock, in whom I take refuge. He is my shield and the horn of my salvation, my stronghold." "As for God, his way is perfect; the word of the Lord is flawless. He is a shield for all who take refuge in him. For who is God besides the Lord? And who is the Rock except our God? It is God who arms me with strength and makes my way perfect." "Surely God is my help; the Lord is the one who sustains me" (Ps. 94:18-19; Ps. 18:2; Ps. 18:30-32; Ps. 54:4 not paraphrased)

Prayers, Praises, and Personal Notes

_____

_____

_____

WEEK TWELVE

Renewed Faith

"In this you greatly rejoice, though now for a little while
you may have had to suffer grief in all kinds of trials.
These have come so that your faith—of greater worth than gold,
which perishes even though refined by fire—
may be proved genuine and may result in
praise, glory and honor when Jesus Christ is revealed."

1 PETER 1:6-7

*G*eri Duncan shares what God accomplished in her life through her husband's battle with Alzheimer's disease. "The harder the trials, the brighter your life can shine for Christ through them. God opened the doors for our son, two daughters, and me to sing and share in the nursing home. We never would have done that on our own. This brought Dave joy; even though he couldn't talk to us, he smiled from ear to ear.

"Jeremiah 29:11 assured us that the plans God had for Dave and me were for good and not for disaster, to give us a hope and a future. He promised to hear our prayers! And the answer through the years was that this was a 'perfect' opportunity to give testimony of the Lord's love and grace through a sad time.

"When we don't have a need, we can't tell how God meets our needs. When we're not alone, we cannot tell how he fills our loneliness. When we are loved by a lover, we cannot really feel and tell how much God loves us in a deep, intimate way. Until we are alone, we have no idea how it feels to be loved so deeply by God. Unless we are in great financial need, we can't testify how God met our need. The list goes on and on.

"Our testimony can be greater when we are in great need. How often do we look for the blessings in tragedy? We take far too much in our lives for granted. It helped me immensely when I focused on the small daily blessings and thanked and praised the Lord for them. Education about Dave's disease and a heart of gratitude helped more than anything else outside of God's Word—His love letter to me."

Our faith is renewed in suffering when we discover what the Lord accomplishes through it. We find immense comfort when we realize the many different ways God uses our trials to touch other people's lives.

The Discovery of God

After all of Job's searching for answers, God didn't address any of Job's questions or explain why he suffered. Instead God quizzed Job about his understanding of creation and asked such questions as: "Where were you when I laid the earth's foundation?" (Job 38:4a). "Have you ever given orders to the morning, or shown the dawn its place?" (Job 38:12). "Do you know the laws of the heavens? Can you set up God's dominion over the earth?" (Job 38:33). Why would God question Job in this manner?

We have the answer in Romans. "For what can be known about God is plain to them [everyone], because God has shown it to them. Ever since the creation of the world his eternal power and divine nature, invisible though they are, have been understood and seen through the things he has made" (Rom. 1:19-20a NRSV).

God had made Himself evident to Job. He could clearly see that the created world indicated the existence of a Creator. If Job had understood God's power over the universe, he would have known that God was with him in suffering. In a sense God is saying to Job as He says to us, "You were so focused on your pain and your questions that you could not see Me."

Furthermore, "The Lord said to Job: 'Will the one who contends with the Almighty correct him? Let him who accuses God answer him!'" (Job 40:1-2).

"Then Job answered the Lord: 'I am unworthy—how can I reply to you? I put my hand over my mouth. I spoke once, but I have no answer—twice, but I will say no more'" (Job 40:3-5).

After God spoke, Job realized that he didn't need to know why he had suffered. He needed to hear God's voice. Now Job had the assurance that the Lord had been present with him in his suffering.

God gave Job what he truly needed; God gave Himself, and He has given Himself to us. "What He did was to make his own glory pass before the man; and it is significant that when He did so, Job had no other question to ask," states G. Campbell Morgan in *The Answers of Jesus to Job*.[1] Job discovered God and realized that His presence alone is more than sufficient.

"He came. He entered space and time and suffering. He came, like a lover. Love seeks above all intimacy, presence, togetherness. . . . He came. Job is satisfied even though the God who came gave him absolutely no answers at all to his thousand tortured questions. He did the most important thing, and he gave the most important gift: himself. It is a lover's gift."[2]

Jesus Answers Job

We move into the spiritual renewal phase as we discover God's love through Jesus, who is the answer to all of Job's questions and our own.

During Job's desperate search for God, he was seeking one who could intervene on his behalf. What is so amazing about the boldness of Job's faith and his declarations about God was that He did not have a Bible or the powerful promises of God to comfort him as we do.

Here are Job's declarations and questions that Jesus has answered for us: First, Job cried out that he had no one to represent him. He had no one to make peace between himself and God. "For He is not a man, as I am, that I may answer Him, and that we should go to court together. Nor is there any mediator between us, who may lay his hand on us both" (Job 9:32-33 NKJV). Job begged God to answer his cries for a hearing, so he could discuss his suffering with Him and discover the reasons why.

Jesus our Mediator answers our cry for someone to represent us. "For there is one God; there is also one mediator between God and humankind, Christ Jesus, himself human, who gave himself a ransom for all" (1 Tim. 2:5-6a NRSV).

The man Christ Jesus provided a more personal way to approach God and have an intimate relationship with Him. Jesus gave Himself as a ransom—He paid the price for our sins when He died on the cross. He demonstrated God's love for us by coming to earth as a man and taking the punishment we deserved.

"In summary, Jesus did three things to solve the problem of suffering. First, he came. He suffered with us. He wept."[3] Second, in coming to earth He personally showed how much He cared by healing people and showing them the way to salvation. "Third, he died and rose. Dying, he paid the price for sin and opened heaven to us; rising, he transformed death from a hole into a door, from an end to a beginning."[4] And He guaranteed us a future in heaven without suffering.

Moreover, Jesus came to serve and give Himself for us. "For even the Son of Man did not come to be served, but to serve, and to give his life as a ransom for many" (Mark 10:45). He came to serve us in our suffering. We can be assured of His tender care and the Holy Spirit's comforting, indwelling presence in all of our afflictions.

Job's second bold declaration is quite astounding. "Though he slay me, yet will I hope in him" (Job 13:15a). What a powerful affirmation of Job's confidence in God. "Though He slay me, I will stick to it that God is a God of love and justice and truth. I see no way out at all, but I will remain true to my belief."[5]

Jesus our living Lord answers our fears about death and shows how we can honor Him both in life and death. "I eagerly expect and hope that I will in no way be ashamed, but will have sufficient courage so that now as always Christ will be exalted in my body, whether by life or by death. For to me, to live is Christ and to die is gain" (Phil. 1:20-21).

Living gives us the opportunity to serve Christ in our suffering and to glorify Him. Dying takes us into Christ's presence where we're freed from all pain. What can be more wonderful?

Third, Job questioned, "If a man dies, will he live again?" (Job 14:14a). Job longed for the assurance that there is life with God after death.

Jesus our resurrected Lord answers our need for assurance that we will live forever. "I am the resurrection and the life. He who believes in me will live, even though he dies; and whoever lives and believes in me will never die" (John 11:25-26).

We can be certain that this life is not all there is, that death is but a dark journey into a heavenly place. Death is the last enemy, but it cannot harm us; through it we are carried into Christ's presence. G. Campbell Morgan reminds us that if anything makes our suffering bearable, it is the assurance that we will continue living even though we daily draw closer to death.[6]

Fourth, Job went from the despair of fearing death and thinking he had no mediator to the hope that someone would testify on his behalf. "Even now my witness is in heaven; my advocate is on high" (Job 16:19).

Jesus our Advocate is our witness before His Father. "For Christ . . . entered into heaven itself, now to appear in the presence of God on our behalf" (Heb. 9:24 NRSV). We have this comforting assurance that He is our witness who testifies for us when we come into the presence of the Father. "We have one who speaks to the Father in our defense—Jesus Christ, the Righteous One" (1 John 2:1b).

Fifth, Job declared that his witness in heaven was interceding in prayer for him. "My intercessor is my friend as my eyes pour out tears to God; on behalf of a man he pleads with God as a man pleads for his friend" (Job 16:20-21).

Jesus our Friend answers our cry for an intercessor. "Christ Jesus, who died—more than that, who was raised to life—is at the right hand of God and is also interceding for us" (Rom. 8:34). No matter how painful life gets, we have this assurance that Jesus is concerned about us. He has not forgotten us. He is not only our witness, but He does even more; He intercedes for us regarding our troubles and trials. He speaks to the Father for us when we have no words to express our deepest heartaches.

Sixth, Job proclaimed, "I know that my Redeemer lives, and that in the end he will stand upon the earth. And after my skin has been destroyed, yet in my flesh I will see God; I myself will see him with my own eyes!" (Job 19:25-27a).

Job's proclamation that "my Redeemer lives" was not only powerfully prophetic but personally significant to Job. A redeemer in Jewish society was the closest male relative, whom God appointed to be the defender of oppressed family members in dire need. If a widow lost the property she inherited because she couldn't pay her debts, the redeemer bought the land and gave it back to her. He was the one who purchased a relative out of slavery and set him or her free. A redeemer could represent a close family member in court and plead his or her case.

"A redeemer was a vindicator of one unjustly wronged. He was a defender of the oppressed. A champion of the suffering. An advocate of one unjustly accused," explains pastor and writer Steven Lawson.[7] But none of Job's closest relatives came forward to be his redeemer, to stand up for him, to avenge the murders of his children, to defend him against false accusers. Job came to the conclusion that only his ever-living Redeemer-God would be his sure defender.

Jesus our Savior answers our need of a Redeemer. "In him we have redemption through his blood, the forgiveness of sins, in accordance with the riches of God's grace that he lavished on us with all wisdom and understanding" (Eph. 1:7-8).

Christ Jesus became flesh and blood so that He could be our Redeemer-Deliverer. He is our next of kin, who paid our debt and set us free. He bought us out of the slavery of sin and paid the price of our suffering, and being freed from both of them is our heavenly inheritance.

Jesus can also redeem our sinful past. When we're delivered from destructive and hurtful attitudes and actions, we walk in newness of life and demonstrate to others that we are changed people. By our testimony of the Lord's transforming work in our lives, He redeems our past and brings glory to

Himself. The Lord also redeems our suffering as we glorify Him by our steadfast faith and share the ways He comforts and supports us in our heartaches.

Furthermore, Job proclaimed that when we die, we will see our Redeemer. We have this hope to look forward to. "Yes, dear friends, we are already God's children, and we can't even imagine what we will be like when Christ returns. But we do know that when he comes we will be like him, for we will see him as he really is" (1 John 3:2 NLT).

Spiritual Victory

Satan attempted to debate one question with God: Would Job curse God in suffering? Job had no idea that he and his faith were that important in the heavenly and earthly realms. He didn't realize that his spiritual victory had eternal significance.

Our spiritual victory is not only a testimony to others here on earth but to unseen witnesses as well. We have important choices to make regarding the trying of our faith, for others on earth and in heaven are watching how we respond to our afflictions.

Job was not aware of what we know: God, a host of heavenly beings, and Satan were watching him—as they are us. "Therefore, since we are surrounded by such a great cloud of witnesses, let us throw off everything that hinders and the sin that so easily entangles, and let us run with perseverance the race marked out for us. Let us fix our eyes on Jesus, the author and perfecter of our faith, who for the joy set before him endured the cross, scorning its shame, and sat down at the right hand of the throne of God. Consider him who endured such opposition from sinful men, so that you will not grow weary and lose heart" (Heb. 12:1-3).

Edith Schaeffer comments on these verses: "This description of being surrounded with witnesses puts our lives into a kind of stadium where (it seems to me) we are running a race in front of onlookers who have gone before us and care about the outcome of our individual races."

Through Job we gain a glimpse of what is going on in our own lives. We see that the battle over Job and our own lives is waged "in the heavenlies and demonstrates that the action and reaction of a human being has significance in the victory that takes place in the heavenlies. . . . Satan's planned afflictions are aimed at getting the people of God to criticize Him in a variety of ways and in different intensities."[8]

Even though Job didn't criticize God, Satan was certain he could entice

Job to do so when his devilish workers destroyed all that was precious to Job. Instead Job sought after God with all his heart and held on to his faith.

How could Job imagine that his commitment to God in suffering would comfort and minister to untold numbers of sufferers down through the ages? "As an example of suffering and patience, beloved, take the prophets who spoke in the name of the Lord. Indeed we call blessed those who showed endurance. You have heard of the endurance of Job, and you have seen the purpose of the Lord, how the Lord is compassionate and merciful" (James 5:10-11 NRSV).

"Faith must be tried; otherwise it is of no worth to God. Think of the dignity it gives to a man's life to know that God has put His honor in his keeping. Our lives mean more than we can tell; they mean that we are fulfilling some purpose of God about which we know nothing any more than Job did."[9]

The testimony of our life and trust in the Lord is more important than the heartbreaking losses we suffer. Keeping our faith in God during trials as Job did matters for all eternity. We can't begin to imagine how the strength of our faith in affliction encourages others in their commitment to the Lord.

"We are to keep on the course which the Lord lays out for us individually and seek to do His will hour by hour as we follow that course. However, in the midst of it all, we cannot tell what is Satan's sharpest aimed arrow or dart or what is the most important victory. Satan will try to come up and hit us when and where we least expect it, and not only are we in danger of not recognizing the attack as *his* attack, but of not realizing how important our victory is."[10]

"God blesses the people who patiently endure testing. Afterward they will receive the crown of life that God has promised to those who love him" (James 1:12 NLT). "We are meant to understand that one very important victory we are meant to have is a series of repeated 'overcomings' in a variety of difficulties."[11]

We often think of victory as overcoming the enemy in war, as an achievement of mastery, success in a struggle against great odds, or winning the game. Victory in God's sight is not winning or achieving success, but it is spiritually overcoming in affliction by trusting and loving Him.

"We are individuals with significance in history, so immensely important that no one else can live our lives or die our deaths for us. No one else can have our joys or bear our pain for us. It is not possible for anyone else to win our victories for us in any area."[12]

That is the real victory, loving the Lord when our life is the bleakest, when we're hurting deeply and nothing makes sense. We often want God to meet our needs, but how often do we desire to be a blessing to Him? We are victorious when we continue to trust Him even when things grow worse.

Geri shared how the Lord helped her gain spiritual victory when she was ready to give up. "I went through a very low time of feeling inadequate to the task the Lord had given Dave and me. I felt I couldn't function alone, and I couldn't. I went to my boss and asked him to relieve me of my position as Prayer Ministries Director. I didn't feel I had enough knowledge to do the business end of things that needed to be done. I also learned that I'd always leaned heavily on my husband to do those things. I needed the Lord's help and to lean more heavily on Him. Now was the time for me to learn about *real* faith in the Lord.

"That's when the Lord reminded me of Hebrews 12, about running the race with perseverance as the cloud of witnesses stood by and watched—and not giving up! The Lord helped me through all the processes in the ministry to get the tasks completed. Even today when I read some of the papers I've written, I'm amazed that I wrote them. I realize the Holy Spirit is the one who worked through me."

Glorifying God in Suffering

Finally, our chief purpose in suffering is to glorify God. We can cry out triumphantly, "I consider that our present sufferings are not worth comparing with the glory that will be revealed in us" (Rom. 8:18).

"Wherefore glorify ye the Lord in the fires, even the name of the Lord God of Israel" (Isa. 24:15 KJV). "We are to honor Him in the trial—in that which is an affliction. . . . But just here we are to glorify Him by our perfect faith in His goodness and love that has permitted all this to come upon us. And more than that, we are to believe that out of this is coming something more for His praise than could have come but for the fiery trial."[13]

"In this you greatly rejoice, though now for a little while you may have had to suffer grief in all kinds of trials. These have come so that your faith—of greater worth than gold, which perishes even though refined by fire—may be proved genuine and may result in praise, glory and honor when Jesus Christ is revealed" (1 Pet. 1:6-7).

Scripture Reading: Hebrews 12:1-3

Practicing the Spiritual Life

Since we are surrounded by witnesses, what are we encouraged to do to keep from losing heart?

_____

_____

_____

In what areas of your life do you need to run with perseverance the race marked out for you, with your eyes fixed on Jesus?

_____

_____

_____

Prayer

Jesus, I'll remember that in a race everyone runs, but only one person gets the prize. I also must run in such a way that I will win. I will consider it pure joy whenever I face trials of many kinds, because I know that the testing of my faith develops perseverance. Perseverance must finish its work so that I may be mature and complete, not lacking anything. Then I can say, "I have fought a good fight, I have finished the race, and I have remained faithful. And now the prize awaits me—the crown of righteousness that the Lord, the righteous Judge, will give me on that great day of his return. And the prize is not just for me but for all who eagerly look forward to his glorious return." (1 Cor. 9:24 NLT; James 1:2-4; paraphrased; 2 Tim. 4:7-8 NLT not paraphrased)

Prayers, Praises, and Personal Notes

_____

_____

_____

Scripture Reading: 1 Peter 1:6-7

Practicing the Spiritual Life

What can suffering and trials do for us spiritually? How valuable is our faith?

_____

_____

_____

_____

Through what trying situations has your faith been refined?

_____

_____

_____

_____

Prayer

Sovereign Lord, You have refined me, but not like silver; You have tested me in the furnace of adversity. Therefore, I will keep alert, stand firm in my faith, be courageous and strong. How much better to get wisdom than gold, to choose understanding rather than silver! Now may I always be filled with the fruit of Your salvation—those good things that are produced in my life by You, Jesus Christ—for this will bring much glory and praise to You, O God. (Isa. 48:10 NRSV; 1 Cor. 16:13 NRSV; Prov. 16:16; Phil. 1:11 NLT, all paraphrased)

Prayers, Praises, and Personal Notes

_____

_____

_____

_____

Scripture Reading: Job 9:32-35; 1 Timothy 2:5-6

Practicing the Spiritual Life

Whom did Job think he needed and why?

_____

_____

What does Christ Jesus do for us? For what did He give Himself?

_____

_____

During what fearful trials have you felt the need for a mediator or someone to speak for you and present your concerns to God?

_____

_____

Prayer

O Christ, You are the mediator of a new covenant, that I who am called may receive the promised eternal inheritance—now that You have died as a ransom to set me free from my sins. Son of Man, You did not come to be served, but to serve, and to give Your life as a ransom for many. Therefore, "You do see! Indeed you note trouble and grief, that you may take it into your hands." "You both precede and follow me. You place your hand of blessing on my head. Such knowledge is too wonderful for me, too great for me to know!" (Heb. 9:15; Matt. 20:28 paraphrased; Ps. 10:14a NRSV; Ps. 139:5-6 NLT not paraphrased)

Prayers, Praises, and Personal Notes

_____

_____

_____

Scripture Reading: Job 13:15-16; Philippians 1:20-21

Practicing the Spiritual Life

Where did Job put his hope, what did he believe he would be able to do, and how did he think it would turn out?

_____

_____

_____

In what areas of your life do you need to put your hope in Christ and have the courage to honor Him, whether by life or by death?

_____

_____

_____

Prayer

Through suffering, this body of mine constantly shares in Your death, Jesus, so that Your life may also be seen in my body. Yes, I live under constant danger of death because I serve You, so that Your life will be obvious in my dying body. You Yourself bore my sins in Your body on the tree, so that I might die to sins and live for righteousness; by Your wounds I have been healed. Therefore, I do not live to myself, and I do not die to myself. If I live, I live to You, Lord, and if I die, I die to You; so then, whether I live or whether I die, I am Yours, Lord. (2 Cor. 4:10-11 NLT; 1 Peter 2:24; Rom. 14:7-8 NRSV, all paraphrased)

Prayers, Praises, and Personal Notes

_____

_____

_____

Scripture Reading: Job 14:14; John 11:25-26

Practicing the Spiritual Life

What assurance did Job long for?

_____

_____

_____

How can Jesus' assurance strengthen your faith?

_____

_____

_____

Prayer

Just as You, Christ, were raised from the dead by the glory of the Father, even so I also should walk in newness of life. For if I have been united with You, Jesus, in the likeness of Your death, certainly I also shall be in the likeness of Your resurrection. As a result, I can really know You and experience the mighty power that raised You from the dead. I can learn what it means to suffer with You, sharing in Your death. Praise be to God, the Father of my Lord Jesus Christ! In Your great mercy You have given me new birth into a living hope, through Jesus' resurrection from the dead. (Rom. 6:4b-5 NKJV; Phil. 3:10 NLT; 1 Peter 1:3, all paraphrased)

Prayers, Praises, and Personal Notes

_____

_____

_____

_____

Scripture Reading: Job 16:19-21; Hebrews 9:24; Romans 8:34

Practicing the Spiritual Life

What does Jesus do for us?

_____

_____

_____

In what ways does it comfort you to know that Jesus is your advocate and is interceding for you?

_____

_____

_____

Prayer

Jesus Christ, the Righteous One, if I sin, I have You who will speak to the Father in my defense. Therefore, O God, You are able once and forever to save me. I come to You through Christ Jesus, for He lives forever to plead with You on my behalf. And, Holy Spirit, You help me in my distress. For I don't even know what I should pray for, nor how I should pray. But You pray for me with groanings that I cannot express in words. And, Father, You who know my heart know what the Holy Spirit is saying, for He pleads for me in harmony with Your own will. (1 John 2:1b; Heb. 7:25 NLT; Rom. 8:26-27 NLT, all paraphrased)

Prayers, Praises, and Personal Notes

_____

_____

_____

Scripture Reading: Job 19:25-27; Ephesians 1:7-8

Practicing the Spiritual Life

What does our Redeemer promise us?

_____

_____

_____

In what ways has your faith been strengthened as you've discovered the different ways Jesus your Redeemer cares for you and presents your needs to His Father?

_____

_____

_____

Prayer

Almighty God, You have rescued me from the dominion of darkness and brought me into the kingdom of the Son You love, in whom I have redemption, the forgiveness of my sins. Yes, God, I am already Your child, and I can't even imagine what I will be like when You return, Jesus Christ my Savior. But I do know that when You come, I will be like You, for I will see You as You really are. I put my hope in You, for with You is unfailing love, and with You is full redemption. (Col. 1:13-14; 1 John 3:2 NLT; Ps. 130:7, all paraphrased)

Prayers, Praises, and Personal Notes

_____

_____

_____

WEEK THIRTEEN

Serve with Compassion

*"Praise be to the God and Father of our Lord Jesus Christ,
the Father of compassion and the God of all comfort,
who comforts us in all our troubles,
so that we can comfort those in any trouble
with the comfort we ourselves have received from God."*

2 CORINTHIANS 1:3-4

*T*hrough our own suffering God gives us "divine appointments" to minister to others. My friend Geri Duncan said, "All through my husband's illness I was learning about brain diseases and how to care for him. I hoped that what I learned would enable me to help others in some way. God has given me many opportunities to pray for and encourage people who have spouses or parents suffering from Alzheimer's or other brain diseases. I spend a lot of time with two women who feel that their husbands don't understand their emotional needs as they grieve through the living deaths of their parents.

"My children and I also witnessed by song and testimony in hospitals and the nursing home that Dave was in. We were given six Christmas holidays to sing carols in the halls. We sang other times, too, especially on Father's Day. We had many opportunities that came only because of Dave's illness."

Giving and Receiving Spiritual Comfort

We grow in our faith through grief and as we move through the spiritual reaction, rebuilding, and renewal phases. In doing so, we have the opportunity to fulfill the Lord's purposes for our suffering, which is to serve others with compassion. Because of our trials we have opportunities to comfort other hurting people. Moreover, Jesus works for His good and His glory as we demonstrate our trust in Him.

People may become Christians because of our testimony and steadfast love for the Lord in trials. There are also those who come to know Christ as Savior because they realize their spiritual need when they suffer.

Many Christians have a ministry they never expected to have because of an affliction, hardship, or loss. God has given Ron and me many opportunities to comfort others because of the heartaches we've been through. Ron has been an encourager to men going through heart surgery.

In 2 Corinthians 1:3-7 we discover the spiritual basis for finding and giving comfort. "All praise to the God and Father of our Lord Jesus Christ. He is the source of every mercy and the God who comforts us" (2 Cor. 1:3 NLT). We are consoled in our sorrow as we offer sacrificial praise to our Lord. As we thank Him for being a Father of compassion and mercy, for calming our fears and troubled minds, He fills us with joy and peace.

Being thankful, however, is not a way to persuade God to free us from suffering. Praise is a pure, sacrificial offering to the Lord in our pain.

"He comforts us in all our troubles so that we can comfort others" (2 Cor. 1:4a NLT). God comforts us in all our afflictions and tribulations—not just some of them. All means completely, entirely, wholly. God gives His all to us. But are we willing to receive all that He has to give us? Are we missing out on God's supportive presence because we're determined to handle our own problems or we want Him to care for us in a certain way?

Our ever-loving Comforter who dwells within us is always caring for us. But we may not feel His presence because of our sorrow or our mood, or we're too focused on what we want. We experience His presence as we talk to Him with the assurance that He is always with us and loves more than any other human being could love us.

The Lord promised, "As a mother comforts her child, so will I comfort you" (Isa. 66:13). We need to run to our Comforter and let Him cradle us in His arms. Let us come to His Word for encouragement and support and open our hearts to the Spirit's constant reassurance.

"When others are troubled, we will be able to give them the same comfort God has given us" (2 Cor 1:4b NLT). In suffering the Holy Spirit is with us, upholding us. As He sustains us and soothes our broken hearts, He is also teaching us how to be a comforter. As we avail ourselves of His caring support, we discover how to be there for others in the same way.

"You can be sure that the more we suffer for Christ, the more God will shower us with his comfort through Christ" (2 Cor. 1:5 NLT). The more we suffer, the more our ability to comfort overflows and abounds to others through Jesus who suffered for us. Those who suffer much have much to give; their lives are rich in sorrow but even richer in comfort because they have an intimate relationship with the Comforter of their souls.

Though our Comforter is often silent, it is a caring quietness that brings peace to a broken heart. "It is this: *recognizing* that Presence unseen, so wondrous and quieting, so soothing and calming and warming. *Recognize His* presence—the Master's own. He is here, close by; His presence is real."[1]

"So when we are weighed down with troubles, it is for your benefit and salvation! For when God comforts us, it is so that we, in turn, can be an encouragement to you. Then you can patiently endure the same things we suffer" (2 Cor. 1:6 NLT).

"Let us be more careful to learn all the lessons in the school of sorrow than we are anxious for the hour of deliverance. There is a 'need-be' for every lesson, and when we are ready, our deliverance will surely come, and we shall find that we could not have stood in our place of higher service without the very things that were taught us in the ordeal."[2]

Let us not look only at the way our trials affect us, but at how they can spiritually benefit and help others. As we faithfully rely on the Lord for comfort, we encourage others to bear with patience the same kinds of trials we're experiencing.

"We are confident that as you share in suffering, you will also share God's comfort" (2 Cor. 1:7 NLT). Notice how often the word *comfort* was repeated in this passage. See how many different ways the apostle Paul emphasized the promise of God's care and our need to share the Lord's comfort with one another.

Why did Paul make this urgent plea? Because he who suffered so much was upheld and supported by the Lord and other Christians. But Paul also knew the deep hurt of being abandoned, betrayed, and deserted by Christians. That's why he so strongly urged them to comfort one another. Paul was also assuring them that if other Christians failed them, they surely would be cared for by the Lord.

Ministering to Hurting People

Thoughtful acts of kindness show that we care and help to soften people's trials. Here are some ways we can comfort and encourage others:

Visit hurting people of all ages, remembering teens and children, too. Keep your visit brief, fifteen to thirty minutes at the most. Be sensitive to the person's condition, watching for cues of tiredness or that he or she just needs to be quiet and not talk.

Regularly phone people. Keep your calls brief, listen, and let them talk. Sometimes we avoid calling because the person wants to talk for a long time. Set a time limit up front and then kindly end the conversation when you need to go.

Always affirm that you were glad to talk to or visit with people.

Affirmation is a gift that we need to give often. Thank hurting people for how they have ministered to you, blessed your life, or helped you in some way. When people are suffering, they are insecure and need genuine compliments more than ever. Mention their positive qualities, talents, and gifts. Express appreciation to people for simple things, such as how much their smile lifts your spirits.

Take a small gift such as a comforting booklet about the person's loss or need, flowers, or freshly baked cookies or muffins. One person brought me mini-loaves of different fruit breads with Scripture cards tucked in each one.

Give or send cards or computer E-mail notes. Most often hurting people don't remember what we say to them, but they can read words of comfort again and again. Sending cards to people in our church that we don't know or have a limited acquaintance with means a lot to them, especially when we let them know we are praying and we actually do so. They feel as if the Lord is speaking to other people's hearts about their needs.

One friend sends comforting greeting cards with another small card inside that has a Scripture gem or prayer on it. I have several such cards on my desk; I read them periodically when I need spiritual encouragement.

One church we belonged to has an encourager postcard ministry. Postcards are kept in pew racks. When the pastor mentions special needs and requests, we could immediately write a note and put the postcard in the offering plate. Then the church secretary addressed and mailed the cards.

Remember that anniversaries, birthdays, graduations, holidays, weddings, and other special occasions can be painful for people who have suffered a significant loss. On those occasions send an "I am thinking about you" card with a comforting note.

After my father died, I called my mother on his birthday, their wedding anniversary, and the date of his death. It meant a lot to her to talk about Dad and express her grief.

Form share-and-care prayer groups. One of the greatest helps to me in getting through trying times and growing in my faith is having prayer partners. I meet with one person weekly and others twice a month.

Help start a Christian recovery group for people dealing with divorce, a terminal illness, the loss of a job, the death of a loved one, an eating disorder, or substance addiction; those who need support because a loved one is addicted or has a mental or physical disability or illness; or people going through life-changing trials of any kind.

Geri said, "One thing that helped a lot was the good friendships I developed with three Christian women who attended the Alzheimer's support group. All of us had husbands when we met eight years ago, and one by one the Lord took the men home. I still meet with those friends every few months for dinner at a restaurant where we catch up on our lives and encourage each other."

If people express a desire for information about their particular need, assist them in finding reading materials (check the public library), educational workshops, support groups, and community services. Geri told how those resources helped her and Dave:

"The Lord allowed us to be accepted into the Medicare Alzheimer's Project for a full year. They gave me twenty-seven hours per month of any kind of help I wanted in the home. This allowed me to work in our regional office one day a week while the caregiver watched Dave and did housework and cooking. This service was so helpful, and I knew the Lord provided it."

Offer care for people with ongoing needs. Many people who have diseases, disabilities, low incomes, or a series of heartbreaking losses are doing the best they can to solve those problems, but they can't do it alone.

One church we belonged to had a care ministry board that set up different kinds of support ministries. Members went through extensive training to become lay care ministers. Each caregiver made a one-year commitment to meet weekly with and assist a hurting person.

The church developed many T.L.C. (tender loving care) small groups for spiritual growth, prayer, recovery from addictions, grief support, and coping with other kinds of losses or trials. They also organized a monthly food distribution through a national organization where low-income families, single parents, and elderly people in the church and community could buy, for example, eighty dollars worth of groceries for thirty.

Finally, realize your own limitations in helping others. Many people's problems are so serious that they need the help of a pastor or Christian counselor. Gently guide people in that direction if they're open to it.

Listening

Who comforts us the most? The person who has been through the valley of suffering and knows how to listen quietly with an open heart. Without the person even speaking, we can feel a Spirit-filled compassion and understanding. She has carried her own cross, and she knows how to help you carry yours without nailing you to it. We need to follow that same example when listening to those who are suffering.

Listen. Listen. Listen. Let the other person do most of the talking. Pointless chatter and talking about everything else but the person's need is not comforting to him or her; it's draining and exhausting. It makes the person feel you are avoiding his or her concerns, and that causes resentment.

Give your full attention to the person when you're listening. Notice both the person's spoken and unspoken communication. Show that you're listening by keeping eye contact and offering appropriate responses. If you fidget, look away, or seem distracted, the person will feel that you don't care and don't want to listen. Then he or she will shut down.

Listen to the person's voice and notice body language. Some people show pain in their eyes, facial expression, and gestures of defeat even as they smile and praise the Lord. "It is important to listen carefully to the hidden message a person expresses as well as to the surface content of what he or she says. . . . It's true that words are used to conceal as well as to reveal. Often a person who is isolated and hurting will use words to mask the pain."[3]

Encourage people to talk about their loss or the person who is causing concern or has passed away. Accept whatever feelings they express, such as anger, bitterness, and shock. Don't correct or criticize people for what they feel or change the subject, thinking it will help them get their mind off their problems. People are often irrational in their grief and need to vent their feelings until they can gain a balanced perspective.

Show empathy when people cry, because it helps them work through and release their grief. Don't be afraid of your own tears; it comforts people when you cry with them.

Allow for long silences. Some people need us to be with them, but they don't feel like talking. An example of this kind of need is when people are at a hospital waiting because they or a loved one is critically ill or going through medical procedures. It means so much to have someone with them, even if you just read, walk around together, or go get snacks.

What to Say and Not to Say

Refrain from offering easy answers. "Life is complicated. . . . Little happens in life that can be adequately explained by one simple answer or Scripture verse. Many losses remain a secret to God on this side of eternity. . . . Never be afraid to admit you don't have all the answers."[4]

Be careful not to assume you understand what people are trying to say and jump in with an answer before they can complete their thoughts. When people are hurting, they often start out slowly and need time to sort through their feelings and deal with the impact of their loss. As people hear themselves talking about their concerns, painful reality and new realizations often strike them.

Give advice only when it's asked for. Listening with compassion, without giving advice, is the kindest gift we can give hurting people. Most people won't welcome our telling them what they should do or how to solve their problems.

If we aren't close to the situation, we rarely have a clear picture, understand the dynamics of the situation, know all the personalities involved, or recognize the ability or inability of people to deal with their problems. We also make others feel that they're incompetent to make decisions when we keep telling them what they should do.

Even when people do ask for advice, we need to assist them in making their own decisions. We can't solve other people's problems, but we can support them and encourage them to find their own solutions. Some people need to think of all the options, even ones that won't work, before they can come to a balanced conclusion about what to do.

Help them think of possible solutions. For example: "What do you think you need to do to deal with this situation?" "What options have you thought of?"

Avoid making judgmental comments such as: "You shouldn't feel that way." "Where's your faith?" "You're overreacting." "Don't be so negative."

Here are some suggestions as to what to say and what not to say when ministering to others.

What you can say:

"I care for you and will be here for you."

"I'm praying for you."

"I'm going to miss (name)." If you were close to the person who passed away, share your own memories and how much the person meant to you.

Most of the time you don't need to say anything. Listening and being with the person is enough.

What not to say:

"I know how you feel."

"What you should do is . . ."

"You're a strong person; you'll get through it."

"She's better off now." The person who is left behind may not feel better off.

"Come and see me." Or "Call me when you need to talk." The person won't.

"I understand. I've been through the same thing." Then you launch into your own story.

"I know someone who has it far worse than you." Then you tell how bad off that person is.

Hurting people especially need to know that God loves them and cares for them, but the following remarks will cause them to question His care:

"It was God's will."

"God doesn't make mistakes."

"It was all a part of God's plan."

"God will give you something (or someone) better."

Here are some other important things to remember when ministering to others:

Ask people how they're doing instead of congratulating them on how "well" they're doing. Hurting people will tell you what you want to hear to comfort you because they feel you can't handle their grief.

Put aside your own concerns so you don't burden hurting people with your heartaches. Don't expect them to comfort you or take care of your emotional or physical needs.

Refrain from telling people how well you handle heartaches in order to give them an example of how they should cope.

Don't assume what people feel about any kind of loss; let them tell you. Sarah said, "When my aunt passed away, someone who didn't know her said to me, 'She is in a far better place.' I didn't know what to say because my aunt had always insisted—even as she was dying—that she didn't believe in God and was convinced she would cease to exist after death."

Refrain from preaching sermons, praising the Lord for the person's suffering and opportunity to glorify God, or quoting verses, especially: "And we know that in all things God works for the good of those who love him, who have been called according to his purpose" (Rom. 8:28).

A friend of mine said that when her family was going through a series of heavy trials, Christians often quoted that verse to her. She felt as if they were saying that if she loved the Lord enough, things would work out for her family's good. She felt spiritually inferior and wondered what the family was doing wrong, even though they were doing the best they could to deal with their problems.

Practical Ways to Serve with Compassion

Here are some practical ways to serve hurting people—baby-sit, clean, do laundry, shop for groceries or other needed items, take a car to be repaired or serviced, or do any other needed chore. If you have the expertise and people ask for help, assist them in taking care of financial matters. Some people need an advocate to get them proper medical care. Help people sort through doctor bills and fill out medical insurance forms, which can be an overwhelming task.

Provide meals; bring food in disposable containers. Put prepared meals in plastic bags so they can be frozen until they're needed. Remember to check for diet restrictions; for example, diabetics can't have high-sugar foods.

Geri shared the many practical ways people helped her and Dave. When he became ill, their supervisors at Wycliffe Bible Translators felt it was best for Dave and Geri to move from California to their home in Oregon.

The people from their church in California and Wycliffe coworkers boxed up their belongings and loaded a rental truck. Dave's brother and brother-in-law drove the truck to Oregon.

In Oregon their church family painted every room in their house, which had been a rental and needed to be refurbished. Someone paid for and picked out new carpeting for every room. They unloaded the truck, unpacked boxes, set up furniture, made the bed, and stocked cupboards with groceries and staples. Later fourteen men from a Sunday school class put up a new fence around the house.

Their Wycliffe and church families provided meals for two months. Some of Geri's friends took her out for little breaks while their husbands, Dave's friends, would sit with him. When Dave improved for a period of time, his friends took him out for coffee.

Geri was also grateful that Wycliffe let her manage the prayer ministries from home. Geri said, "The Lord went ahead of us and provided every service we needed before we'd ask, even needed finances through an anonymous donor." The last year before Dave went to the nursing home, their church family brought meals again and took Geri places to get her out of the house.

Dave's sister and husband took Geri on a cruise for a vacation. She said, "They assured me it was okay to laugh and have fun again and not feel guilty that Dave could not be with us. That vacation helped me more than anything. It didn't need to be a cruise; it could have been a vacation to anywhere with them. It was just their attitude that did it. They made me feel special and loved. I knew they wanted God's best for my life, and they were trying to meet a need."

Many Christians working together can make a big difference in helping hurting people get through difficult trials. It's not just the major things we do to help, but there are many small ways we can show we care—as Judie Frank shares in her poem.

THE PHONE CALL

I needed some encouragement not so long ago,
when a special friend of mine called to say hello.
She didn't know I was discouraged and feeling blue.
She only called to say, "Hi," and talk a minute or two.
We spent a few minutes talking about our day.
Then I said my heart was heavy and needed her to pray.
I shared my problems with her and my deepest cares;
My burdens grew lighter as she lifted me up in prayer.
It was just a little phone call in the middle of the day.
Yet it encouraged me more than words could ever say.[5]

Scripture Reading: 2 Corinthians 1:3-5

Practicing the Spiritual Life

For what can we praise the Lord?

_____

_____

_____

What will you specifically do this week to comfort someone?

_____

_____

_____

Prayer

"Sing for joy, O heavens, and exult, O earth; break forth, O mountains, into singing! For the Lord has comforted his people, and will have compassion on his suffering ones." "Blessed be the Lord, for He has shown me His marvelous kindness!" "This is my comfort in my distress, that your promise gives me life." Therefore, O God, as Your chosen person, holy and dearly loved, I will clothe myself with compassion, kindness, humility, gentleness and patience. (Isa. 49:13 NRSV; Ps. 31:21 NKJV; Ps. 119:50 NRSV not paraphrased; Col. 3:12 paraphrased)

Prayers, Praises, and Personal Notes

_____

_____

_____

_____

Scripture Reading: 2 Corinthians 1:6-9

Practicing the Spiritual Life
What did Paul see as God's purpose in this trial?

_____

_____

_____

Write about a trying time when you and another person/s shared in each other's suffering and comfort.

_____

_____

_____

Prayer

Now as Your child, I am an heir—heir of God and co-heir with You, Christ, if indeed I share in Your sufferings in order that I may also share in Your glory. I consider that my present sufferings are not worth comparing with the glory that will be revealed in me. And You said, 'Comfort, comfort My people.' I will rejoice with those who rejoice, mourn with those who mourn. "I will turn their mourning into joy, I will comfort them, and give them gladness for sorrow." (Rom. 8:17-18; Isa. 40:1; Rom. 12:15 paraphrased; Jer. 31:13b NRSV not paraphrased)

Prayers, Praises, and Personal Notes

_____

_____

_____

Scripture Reading: Acts 16:22-34

Practicing the Spiritual Life

How did Paul and Silas minister to the jailer despite their severe trials?

_____

_____

How was the jailer's life changed, and what did he do to care for Paul and Silas?

_____

_____

How has your faith been changed by trials, and in what ways have you witnessed to others because of what the Lord has done in your life?

_____

_____

Prayer

You are the Lord; You have called me in righteousness, You have taken me by the hand and kept me; You have given me as a covenant to the people, a light to the nations, to open the eyes that are blind, to bring out the prisoners from the dungeon, from the prison those who sit in darkness. "This is right and is acceptable in the sight of God our Savior, who desires everyone to be saved and to come to the knowledge of the truth." For "there is salvation in no one else! There is no other name in all of heaven for people to call on to save them." (Isa. 42:6-7 NRSV paraphrased; 1 Tim. 2:3-4 NRSV; Acts 4:12 NLT not paraphrased)

Prayers, Praises, and Personal Notes

_____

_____

_____

Scripture Reading: Acts 9:36-42

Practicing the Spiritual Life

For what ministries of compassion was Tabitha (Dorcas) known?

_____

_____

When she was raised from the dead, what impact did it have on many of the people?

_____

_____

Name several Christians you know who are always doing good and blessing others. Send them appreciation notes.

_____

_____

Prayer

O ever-giving Lord, I must be an example to others by doing good deeds of every kind. May I learn to maintain good works, to meet urgent needs, that I may not be unfruitful. Equip me with everything good for doing Your will, and may You work in me what is pleasing to You, through Jesus Christ, to whom be glory for ever and ever. Amen. (Titus 2:7a NLT; Titus 3:14 NKJV; Heb. 13:21, all paraphrased)

Prayers, Praises, and Personal Notes

_____

_____

_____

_____

_____

Scripture Reading: Philippians 4:14-20

Practicing the Spiritual Life

In what way did the Philippians minister to Paul? How many other churches helped him?

_____

_____

What did Paul say in blessing the Philippians for their gift?

_____

_____

Make a specific commitment to give your time or a financial or material gift to meet the need of a servant of the Lord.

_____

_____

Prayer

O God, I will be an imitator of You as Your dearly loved child and live a life of love, just as You, Christ, loved me and gave Yourself up for me as a fragrant offering and sacrifice to God. For if I spend myself on behalf of the hungry and satisfy the needs of the oppressed, then my light will rise in the darkness, and my night will become like the noonday. But when I give to the needy, I won't let my left hand know what my right hand is doing, so that my giving may be in secret. Then, Father, You who see what is done in secret, will reward me. Now I want to excel also in this gracious ministry of giving. If I serve You, Christ, with this attitude, I will please God. (Eph. 5:1-2; Isa. 58:10; Matt. 6:3-4; 2 Cor. 8:7b NLT; Rom. 14:18a NLT, all paraphrased)

Prayers, Praises, and Personal Notes

_____

_____

_____

Scripture Reading: Luke 10:25-37

Practicing the Spiritual Life

In what ways did the Samaritan go out of his way to care for the wounded man?

_____

_____

_____

Today make a commitment to show God's love to a person to whom you wouldn't ordinarily reach out.

_____

_____

_____

Prayer

"The Spirit of the Sovereign Lord is on me, because the Lord has anointed me to preach good news to the poor. He has sent me to bind up the brokenhearted, to proclaim freedom for the captives and release from darkness for the prisoners, to proclaim the year of the Lord's favor and the day of vengeance of our God, to comfort all who mourn, and provide for those who grieve in Zion—to bestow on them a crown of beauty instead of ashes, the oil of gladness instead of mourning, and a garment of praise instead of a spirit of despair. They will be called oaks of righteousness, a planting of the Lord for the display of his splendor." (Isa. 61:1-3 not paraphrased)

Prayers, Praises, and Personal Notes

_____

_____

_____

_____

Scripture Reading: Colossians 4:7-18

Practicing the Spiritual Life

List the titles Paul gave the Christians who served with him and the ways they ministered to others.

_____

_____

_____

Give a blessing to hurting people by telling them or sending a note sharing what you appreciate about them or pointing out how they have ministered to you.

_____

_____

_____

Prayer

"How beautiful on the mountains are the feet of those who bring good news, who proclaim peace, who bring good tidings, who proclaim salvation." How thankful I am to You, Christ Jesus my Lord, for considering me trustworthy and appointing me to serve You. I need to persevere so that when I have done Your will, O God, I will receive what You have promised. Therefore, as Your beloved one, I will be steadfast, immovable, always abounding in Your work, Lord, knowing that my labor for You is not in vain. (Isa. 52:7a not paraphrased; 1 Tim 1:12 NLT; Heb. 10:36; 1 Cor. 15:58 NKJV paraphrased)

Prayers, Praises, and Personal Notes

_____

_____

_____

WEEK FOURTEEN

Remember and Rejoice

*"Be glad and rejoice,
for the Lord has done
great things!"*

JOEL 2:21B NRSV

SPIRITUAL RETREAT AND REMEMBRANCE CEREMONY GUIDE

*T*he purpose of this book is to assist us in building up our faith in trying times. When we've suffered a significant loss, we need to be able to think about those life-changing experiences in a way that helps us move on with our lives.

A special ceremony can help us commemorate such experiences, the healing work the Lord has done in us, and the way we have grown and been strengthened in our faith. We need that crowning touch to honor such meaningful passages in our lives. A "graduation" allows us to celebrate and sends us forth into the future with a renewed sense of purpose.

In our society, we don't have formal or informal ceremonies or special occasions to mark those passages. We do special things to recognize losses, but we don't understand why we need to remember, especially when we want to forget past hurts and be free of our grief.

As an example, many years ago I felt a compelling urge to go to my grandparents' former home, the one my grandfather had built. I had many happy memories of being there, especially of summer vacations and Thanksgiving. I also needed to visit my grandparents' graves and my favorite aunt's, who had committed suicide.

One day my closest friend and I drove several hours to the house and then went to the cemetery. All I did was sit on the grass by my aunt's and grandparents' memorial markers, thought about them, and prayed. Afterward my friend and I walked the nearby beach and had lunch in town. It had been many years since their deaths, but for reasons I didn't understand then, I needed to go on that journey. Now I realize that I was seeking a way to remember what my aunt and grandparents had meant to me, to honor their memories, and to put unfinished grief to rest.

In order to find closure and to affirm life-changing experiences, we may have to create a special observance. I have prepared the spiritual retreat and given ideas for a Remembrance Ceremony to meet that need. We will prepare ourselves for this ceremony during the spiritual retreat.

Though I've chosen to call it a Remembrance Ceremony, depending on your own needs (or if you completed this book with others), you might want to call it a Dedication Service, Memorial Service, Graduation, or Celebration Ceremony.

As you've completed *A Woman's Pilgrimage of Faith*, you have been growing through grief and moving through the spiritual reaction, rebuilding, and renewal phases. The spiritual retreat, "Remember and Rejoice," and the Remembrance Ceremony will give you the opportunity to recall where you were emotionally and spiritually when you started your journey, recognize how far you have come, and see what the Lord has done in your life.

The purpose of a Remembrance Ceremony is to express our feelings outwardly about a loss or losses and note how the trial changed us and our lives. This ceremony affirms that our life-changing experiences have significance, impresses upon us the finality of a loss, and assists us in making necessary adjustments to the changes that have come to us. It also enables us to recognize what we have personally and spiritually gained as we've worked through each part of the grieving-healing process.

A Remembrance Ceremony can be a celebration or graduation that marks our completion of a recovery program or recognition that we have overcome adversity to reach a goal we hadn't dreamed of attaining. It can be a dedication ceremony where we commit ourselves to serving in or starting a new Christian ministry.

It can be a solemn service to remind us of what we don't want to forget and those people we want to remember. After the Oklahoma City bombing many such services were held during the year following that tragedy. Women who have had abortions are helped through their grief by having a memorial service.

Guidelines for a Remembrance Ceremony

A Remembrance Ceremony can be as informal and simple or as formal and well-planned as you desire. It doesn't have to be a ceremony; it can be a simple act that is personally meaningful to you. You may simply want to buy fresh flowers or a plant, balloons, or a collectable item that symbolizes this passage in your life.

If you have this ceremony by yourself, make it a part of the spiritual retreat. During that time, you can prepare for the ceremony by deciding what you want to do, read, or say. Read Scripture that especially ministered to you, or use one of the readings included in Appendix A: "Remembrance Ceremony Readings."

Preparation is as important as the actual ceremony. Make the ceremony as brief or as lengthy as you desire, and choose a special place to hold it.

If you went through this book with others, plan the Remembrance Ceremony together before you hold the spiritual retreat, setting a specific time and place for both. Plan an order of service with different people participating in each part.

Afterwards have a meal or refreshments together; sharing around the table gives everyone an added opportunity to reminisce and/or celebrate. If appropriate, invite family and friends to the ceremony.

You can do a Remembrance Ceremony more than once and in many different ways, depending on the losses and changes that you experience throughout your lifetime. It doesn't have to be elaborate; it can be a spontaneous action that you do whenever you feel the need.

Meaningful Ways to Remember

Make a two-page bulletin or booklet for a keepsake. Include the order of service, who participated, readings, worship hymns and songs, date, time, and place of the ceremony. Have each person write a special memory from the group experiences to include in the booklet.

Ask each person to write a positive comment about others in the group. To make it simple limit each comment to just one or two sentences. Put the name of each person in the group at the top of a sheet of paper and pass it around during a meeting.

Ask everyone to consider one of the following questions in writing the comments. How did the person minister to you in a special way? How has the person made a difference in your life? What qualities do you especially appreciate about the person? Then at the ceremony give each person the paper with the comments about him or her.

Take group pictures and put one in a frame, or make a small album of photos. Give each person a certificate, plaque, flowers, or a small symbolic gift during the ceremony.

Plant flowers or a tree. If you enjoy gardening, set aside a special section of your yard. Put a bench in the garden, plaque, and/or waterfall along with plants and flowers that you love. Start a remembrance journal, writing every good thing that came out of your trials, answered prayers, and ways the Lord has ministered to you, spiritually transformed you, and used you to touch other people's lives, or describe how they've touched yours.

Set up a memorial fund. Begin a ministry or commit to financially supporting a ministry in memory of your loss, recovery, or other life-changing experiences.

Start a new tradition as a remembrance. Once a year on the same date or a certain weekend (such as the first weekend of March) plan a retreat to reassess your life personally and spiritually and commit yourself to the Lord anew. If you met with a group, plan a reunion, spiritual retreat, and Remembrance Ceremony.

Throughout our lifetime anniversaries, birthdays, holidays, and special occasions can bring back fresh grief over a loss. Those are times to have a Remembrance Ceremony or to do something simple and positive as a way of commemorating the event.

Thirty-three years ago my friend Shirlee's young son passed away. Every year on the morning of his birth date, she asks the Lord, "What can I do today to honor Mike's memory?" She said, "That day I am less hurried and more aware and sensitive of other people's needs. Instead of grieving and feeling sorry for myself, I am doing something positive by focusing on others and honoring our son's memory at the same time.

"It also gives me an eternal perspective; it's so very easy to get lost in the rush of passing days. When I look back over the span of years, I see things more from God's perspective and see my life in better balance. You truly see what's important in God's eyes and not your own."

If you are doing the following spiritual retreat as a group, please read Appendix B: "Plans for a Small Group Study and Spiritual Retreat". Suggestions for Responsive Readings are also included in Appendix A: "Remembrance Ceremony Readings."

Now as you begin your spiritual retreat, read the following selections slowly, reflecting on how they relate to your own life and spiritual needs. Ask the Holy Spirit to help you find closure and have a renewed sense of purpose as you move on with your life. Seek the Lord's will regarding how He would have you serve Him and others. Respond to the Spirit with an open heart and open mind, seeking His direction as you plan your Remembrance Ceremony.

SPIRITUAL RETREAT GUIDE

Prepare for the Retreat

Date _____

    Write down any needs, obligations, or worries that are concerning you now. Take a few moments to release them to the Lord.

_____

_____

What are the desires of your heart for this time with the Lord?

_____

_____

What life-changing experiences and losses do you desire to recognize and commemorate during your Remembrance Ceremony?

_____

_____

_____

_____

MORNING QUIET TIME

"Continue securely established and steadfast in the faith,
without shifting from the hope promised by the gospel."
COLOSSIANS 1:23a NRSV

Recreation (10 to 20 minutes)

Write the above passage on an index card or paper. Then as you walk, read and reflect on the verse. As the Holy Spirit speaks to you, keep praying that you will be responsive to the changes He desires to make in your life.

Read and Respond

Find a quiet place for your time with the Lord. Write your responses as you feel the need and after any of the following: "Scripture Reading," "Quiet Listening," and "Responsive Reading."

Scripture Reading: Romans 5:1-5 NLT

"Therefore, since we have been made right in God's sight by faith, we have peace with God because of what Jesus Christ our Lord has done for us. Because of our faith, Christ has brought us into this place of highest privilege where we now stand, and we confidently and joyfully look forward to sharing God's glory. We can rejoice, too, when we run into problems and trials, for we know that they are good for us—they help us learn to endure. And endurance develops strength of character in us, and character strengthens our confident expectation of salvation. And this expectation will not disappoint us. For we know how dearly God loves us, because he has given us the Holy Spirit to fill our hearts with his love."

Practicing the Spiritual Life

How are we made right in God's sight?

_____

_____

What can we look forward to with confidence and joy?

_____

_____

In what ways have you developed spiritual endurance through trials?

_____

_____

How has endurance developed strength of character in you?

_____

_____

How do we know that God dearly loves us?

_____

_____

Prayer

Father God, as Your beloved one, I will be steadfast, immovable, always abounding in Your work, knowing that my labor for You is not in vain. I will continue securely established and steadfast in my faith, without shifting from the hope promised by the Gospel. So then, just as I received You, Christ Jesus my Lord, I will continue to live in You, rooted and built up in You, strengthened in my faith as I was taught, and overflowing with thankfulness.

(1 Cor. 15:58 NKJV; Col. 1:23a NRSV; Col. 2:6-7, all paraphrased)

Quiet Listening (15 to 30 minutes)

As you quiet your thoughts before the Lord, you will battle both outward and inward distractions. Keep persevering; keep bringing your thoughts back to God. Ask Him to help you hear Him and to overcome any thoughts that are not from Him. Then record your responses, confess sins and struggles, and note how you are being spiritually encouraged and renewed in your faith.

> *"But you, dear friends, build yourselves up*
> *in your most holy faith and pray in the Holy Spirit."*
> JUDE 20

Respond

_____

_____

_____

_____

_____

Recreation and Refreshment

Take a brief walk and have a light snack if you need to.

Scripture Reading: Philippians 3:13-14 NLT

"No, dear friends, I am still not all I should be, but I am focusing all my energies on this one thing: Forgetting the past and looking forward to what lies ahead, I strain to reach the end of the race and receive the prize for which God, through Christ Jesus, is calling us up to heaven."

Practicing the Spiritual Life

What past things do you need to let go of and forget so you can put them to rest?

_____

_____

What are you looking forward to as you continue on your pilgrimage of faith?

_____

_____

What is the Lord calling you to do as you run this spiritual race?

_____

_____

Prayer

Ever-living Lord, You said, "Behold, I will create new heavens and a new earth. The former things will not be remembered, nor will they come to mind." "Past troubles will be forgotten and hidden from my eyes." I will surely forget my trouble, recalling it only as waters gone by. I will not call to mind the former things or ponder things of the past. O Lord, You will do something new; now it will spring forth.

(Isa. 65:17, 16b not paraphrased; Job 11:16; Isa. 43:18-19a NAS95 paraphrased)

Quiet Listening (15 to 30 minutes)

> *"Create in me a pure heart, O God,*
> *and renew a steadfast spirit within me."*
> PSALM 51:10

Respond

_____

_____

_____

_____

_____

Refreshment, Recreation and Rest (30 minutes to 1 hour)

If you desire, have lunch, walk, and rest. Relax and enjoy this break. Make it a time of praise, thanksgiving, and worship.

AFTERNOON QUIET TIME

Responsive Reading

(If you desire, use the Responsive Readings along with what you've written as part of your Remembrance Ceremony.) Complete the following blessing by describing how the Lord has redeemed your life and blessed you with His benefits:

Bless the Lord, O my soul, and do not forget all his benefits—who forgives all my iniquity, who heals all my diseases, who redeems my life from destruction, who crowns me with lovingkindness and tender mercies, who satisfies me with good as long as I live.

_____

_____

"Bless the Lord, O my soul: and all that is within me, bless his holy name."

(Ps. 103:2-3 NRSV; Ps. 103:4 NKJV; Ps. 103:5a NRSV paraphrased; Ps. 103:1 KJV not paraphrased)

Quiet Listening (15 to 30 minutes)

> *"And God is able to provide you with every blessing in abundance,*
> *so that by always having enough of everything,*
> *you may share abundantly in every good work."*
> 2 CORINTHIANS 9:8 NRSV

Respond

_____

_____

_____

_____

Responsive Reading

Complete the following prayer by writing your appreciation for what the Lord has done in your life:

O Lord, "I remember the days of old. I ponder all your great works. I think about what you have done."

_____

_____

"O Lord my God, you have done many miracles for us. Your plans for us are too numerous to list. If I tried to recite all your wonderful deeds, I would never come to the end of them."

(Ps. 143:5 NLT; Ps. 40:5 NLT not paraphrased)

Recreation and Refreshment

Take a brief walk and have a light snack if you need to.

Responsive Reading

In view of Your mercy, O God, I will offer my body as a living sacrifice, holy and pleasing to You—this is my spiritual act of worship.

I will not conform any longer to the pattern of this world, but I will be transformed by the renewing of my mind. Then I will be able to test and approve what Your will is—Your good, pleasing, and perfect will.

My love will be genuine; I will hate what is evil and hold fast to what is good. I will love others with mutual affection and show them honor. I will not lag in zeal; I will be ardent in spirit and serve You, Lord. I will rejoice in hope, be patient in suffering, and persevere in prayer.

I will contribute to the needs of the saints and extend hospitality to strangers. I will bless those who persecute me; I will bless and not curse them. I will rejoice with those who rejoice and weep with those who weep. I will rejoice in the Lord always. I will say it again: Rejoice!

(Rom. 12:1-2 NIV; Rom. 12:9-15 NRSV; Phil. 4:4 paraphrased)

Practicing the Spiritual Life

In what ways will you give yourself as a living sacrifice to the Lord?

_____

_____

What will you do to serve others with compassion and contribute to the needs of the saints? Set a specific time period to meet those commitments.

_____

_____

In the days ahead, what do you desire the Lord to do in your life as you seek to serve Him and minister to others?

_____

_____

Quiet Listening (15 to 30 minutes)

> *"Be glad and rejoice, for the Lord*
> *has done great things!"*
> JOEL 2:21b NRSV

Respond

_____

_____

_____

Review and Respond

Read over what you've written in your responses. Has the Lord guided you in a special way through the Scriptures, responsive readings or during your prayers and quiet listening? If so, what has the Lord impressed on your heart and mind?

_____

_____

How has the Lord ministered to you and renewed your faith?

_____

_____

_____

Remembrance Ceremony Plans

Write the date, time, and place for the ceremony.

_____

_____

_____

Write what you plan to do and say and in what order.

_____

_____

_____

_____

_____

_____

_____

_____

_____

_____

_____

_____

_____

_____

A P P E N D I X   A:

Remembrance Ceremony Readings

*C*hoose the prayers and readings you desire to use for a Remembrance Ceremony. You may copy them for a booklet or bulletin used for that purpose.

Readings for Individuals

1. STEADFAST FAITH

Father God, since I have been made right in Your sight by faith, I have peace with You because of what Jesus Christ my Lord has done for me. Because of my faith, Christ, You have brought me into this place of highest privilege where I now stand, and I confidently and joyfully look forward to sharing God's glory. Thanks be to God, who gives me the victory through my Lord Jesus Christ.

As Your beloved one, I will be steadfast, immovable, always abounding in Your work, Lord, knowing that my labor for You is not in vain. I will continue securely established and steadfast in my faith, without shifting from the hope promised by the Gospel. So then, just as I received You, Christ Jesus my Lord, I will continue to live in You, rooted and built up in You, strengthened in my faith as I was taught, and overflowing with thankfulness.

(Rom. 5:1-2 NLT; 1 Cor. 15:57; 1 Cor. 15:58 NKJV; Col. 1:23a NRSV; Col. 2:6-7, all paraphrased)

2. FORGETTING FORMER THINGS

Ever-living Lord, You said, "Behold, I will create new heavens and a new earth. The former things will not be remembered, nor will they come to mind." "Past troubles will be forgotten and hidden from my eyes." I will surely forget my trouble, recalling it only as waters gone by. I will not call to mind the former things, or ponder things of the past. O Lord, You will do something new, now it will spring forth.

(Isa. 65:17, 16b not paraphrased; Job 11:16; Isa. 43:18-19a NAS95 paraphrased)

3. FORGETTING THE PAST AND LOOKING FORWARD

Since I am surrounded by such a great cloud of witnesses, I will throw off everything that hinders and the sin that so easily entangles. I will run with perseverance the race marked out for me. I will fix my eyes on You, Jesus, the author and perfecter of my faith, who for the joy set before You endured the cross, scorning its shame, and sat down at the right hand of the throne of God. I will consider You, Christ, who endured such opposition from sinful people, so that I will not grow weary and lose heart.

"I am still not all I should be, but I am focusing all my energies on this one thing: Forgetting the past and looking forward to what lies ahead, I strain to reach the end of the race and receive the prize for which God, through Christ Jesus, is calling us up to heaven."

In this I greatly rejoice, though now for a little while I may have had to suffer grief in all kinds of trials. These have come so that my faith—of greater worth than gold, which perishes even though refined by fire—may be proved genuine and may result in praise, glory, and honor when You are revealed, Jesus Christ my Lord.

(Heb. 12:1-3 paraphrased; Phil. 3:13-14 NLT not paraphrased; 1 Peter 1:5-7 paraphrased)

4. BLESS THE LORD AND DO NOT FORGET

(Describe how the Lord has blessed you with His benefits in trials; read the Scripture along with what you've written as part of the Remembrance Ceremony.)

Bless the Lord, O my soul, and do not forget all His benefits—who forgives all my iniquity, who heals all my diseases, who redeems my life from destruction, who crowns me with lovingkindness and tender mercies, who satisfies me with good as long as I live.

_____

_____

_____

_____

"Bless the Lord, O my soul: and all that is within me, bless his holy name."
(Ps. 103:2-3 NRSV; Ps. 103:4 NKJV; Ps. 103:5a NRSV paraphrased; Ps. 103:1 KJV not paraphrased)

5. REMEMBER WHAT THE LORD HAS DONE

(Write your appreciation for what the Lord has done; read the Scripture along with what you've written as part of the Remembrance Ceremony.)

O Lord, "I remember the days of old. I ponder all your great works. I think about what you have done."

_____

_____

_____

_____

"O Lord my God, you have done many miracles for us. Your plans for us are too numerous to list. If I tried to recite all your wonderful deeds, I would never come to the end of them."

(Ps. 143:5 NLT; Ps. 40:5 NLT not paraphrased)

6. COMFORT ALL WHO MOURN

"The Spirit of the Sovereign Lord is on me, because the Lord has anointed me to preach good news to the poor. He has sent me to bind up the brokenhearted, to proclaim freedom for the captives and release from darkness for the prisoners, to proclaim the year of the Lord's favor and the day of vengeance of our God, to comfort all who mourn, and provide for those who grieve in Zion—to bestow on them a crown of beauty instead of ashes, the oil of gladness instead of mourning, and a garment of praise instead of a spirit of despair. They will be called oaks of righteousness, a planting of the Lord for the display of his splendor."

(Isa. 61:1-3 not paraphrased)

7. REMEMBERING AND REJOICING

"I will remember the deeds of the Lord; yes, I will remember your miracles of long ago." "They are constantly in my thoughts. I cannot stop thinking about them." "Your principles have been the music of my life throughout the years of my pilgrimage."

"I will rejoice and be glad in Your lovingkindness, Because You have seen my affliction; You have known the troubles of my soul, And You have not given me over into the hand of the enemy; You have set my feet in a large place." You lifted me out of the pit of despair, out of the mud and the mire. You set my feet on solid ground and steadied me as I walked along.

"I will praise you, O Lord, with all my heart; I will tell of all your wonders. I will be glad and rejoice in you; I will sing praise to your name, O Most High."

(Ps. 77:11; Ps. 77:12 NLT; Ps. 119:54 NLT; Ps. 31:7-8 NAS95 not paraphrased; Ps. 40:2 NLT paraphrased; Ps. 9:1-2 not paraphrased)

8. COMMITTED TO SERVE WITH COMPASSION

In view of Your mercy, O God, I will offer my body as a living sacrifice, holy and pleasing to You—this is my spiritual act of worship. I will not conform any longer to the pattern of this world, but I will be transformed by the renewing of my mind. Then I will be able to test and approve what Your will is—Your good, pleasing, and perfect will. (Rom. 12:1-2 NRSV paraphrased)

My love will be genuine; I will hate what is evil and hold fast to what is good. I will love others with mutual affection and show them honor. I will not lag in zeal; I will be ardent in spirit and serve You, Lord. I will rejoice in hope, be patient in suffering, and persevere in prayer. I will contribute to the needs of the saints and extend hospitality to strangers. I will bless those who persecute me; I will bless and not curse them. I will rejoice with those who rejoice, and weep with those who weep. I will rejoice in the Lord always. I will say it again: Rejoice!

(Rom. 12:9-15 NRSV; Phil. 4:4, all paraphrased)

Responsive Readings for Groups

The following Responsive Readings can be said in unison, or the leader reads the first stanza and the people the second, alternating to the end. Or have two groups of people alternate saying the stanzas.

1. STEADFAST FAITH

"Since we have been made right in God's sight by faith, we have peace with God because of what Jesus Christ our Lord has done for us."

"Thanks be to God, who gives us the victory through our Lord Jesus Christ."

"Because of our faith, Christ has brought us into this place of highest privilege where we now stand, and we confidently and joyfully look forward to sharing God's glory."

"Thanks be to God, who gives us the victory through our Lord Jesus Christ."

We will continue securely established and steadfast in our faith, without shifting from the hope promised by the Gospel.

"Thanks be to God, who gives us the victory through our Lord Jesus Christ."

We will be steadfast, immovable, always abounding in the work of the Lord, knowing that our labor is not in vain in the Lord.

"Thanks be to God, who gives us the victory through our Lord Jesus Christ."

We will continue to live in Him, rooted and built up in Christ Jesus our Lord, strengthened in our faith as we were taught, and overflowing with thankfulness.

"Thanks be to God, who gives us the victory through our Lord Jesus Christ."

(Rom. 5:1-2 NLT not paraphrased; 1 Cor. 15:57 NKJV not paraphrased [repeated]; Rom. 5:2 NLT; Col. 1:23a NRSV; 1 Cor. 15:58 NKJV; Col. 2:6-7 paraphrased)

2. FORGETTING THE PAST AND LOOKING FORWARD

Since we are surrounded by such a great cloud of witnesses, we will throw off everything that hinders and the sin that so easily entangles.

We will run with perseverance the race marked out for us.

We will fix our eyes on Jesus, the author and perfecter of our faith, who for the joy set before Him endured the cross, scorning its shame, and sat down at the right hand of the throne of God.

We will consider Christ who endured such opposition from sinful men, so that we will not grow weary and lose heart.

We are still not all we should be, but we are focusing all our energies on this one thing: forgetting the past and looking forward to what lies ahead.

We strain to reach the end of the race and receive the prize for which God, through Christ Jesus, is calling us up to heaven.

In this we greatly rejoice, though now for a little while we may have had to suffer grief in all kinds of trials.

These have come so that our faith—of greater worth than gold, which perishes even though refined by fire—may be proved genuine and may result in praise, glory, and honor when You are revealed, Jesus Christ our Lord.

All: "Now to him who is able to do immeasurably more than all we ask or imagine, according to his power that is at work within us, to him be glory in the church and in Christ Jesus throughout all generations, for ever and ever! Amen."

(Heb. 12:1-3; Phil. 3:13-14 NLT; 1 Peter 1:6-7 paraphrased; Eph. 3:20-21 not paraphrased)

3. FORGETTING FORMER THINGS

Ever-living Lord, You said, "Behold, I will create new heavens and a new earth."

"The former things will not be remembered, nor will they come to mind."

Past troubles will be forgotten and hidden from our eyes.

We will surely forget our trouble, recalling it only as waters gone by.

We will not call to mind the former things or ponder things of the past.

O Lord, You will do something new; now it will spring forth.

(Isa. 65:17 not paraphrased; 65:16b; Job 11:16; Isa. 43:18-19a NAS95 paraphrased)

4. COMFORT ALL WHO MOURN

The spirit of the Lord God is upon us, because the Lord has anointed us.

He has sent us to bring good news to the oppressed.

To bind up the brokenhearted.

To proclaim liberty to the captives and release to the prisoners.

To proclaim the year of the Lord's favor and the day of vengeance of our God.

To comfort all who mourn.

To provide for those who mourn in Zion.

To give them a garland instead of ashes.

The oil of gladness instead of mourning.

The mantle of praise instead of a faint spirit.

They will be called oaks of righteousness.

The planting of the Lord, to display His glory.

(Isa. 61:1-3 NRSV paraphrased)

5. Committed to Serve with Compassion

Leader: "I urge you . . . in view of God's mercy, to offer your bodies as living sacrifices, holy and pleasing to God—this is your spiritual act of worship."

People: *By God's mercy, we will offer our bodies as living sacrifices, holy and pleasing to God—this is our spiritual act of worship.*

Leader: "Do not conform any longer to the pattern of this world, but be transformed by the renewing of your mind. Then you will be able to test and approve what God's will is—his good, pleasing and perfect will."

People: *We will not conform any longer to the pattern of this world, but we will be transformed by the renewing of our minds. Then we will be able to test and approve what God's will is—his good, pleasing and perfect will.*

Leader: "Let love be genuine; hate what is evil, hold fast to what is good."

People: *Our love will be genuine; we will hate what is evil and hold fast to what is good.*

Leader: "Love one another with mutual affection."

People: *We will love one another with mutual affection.*

Leader: "Do not lag in zeal, be ardent in spirit, serve the Lord."

People: *We will not lag in zeal; we will be ardent in spirit and serve the Lord.*

Leader: "Rejoice in hope, be patient in suffering, persevere in prayer."

People: *We will rejoice in hope, be patient in suffering, and persevere in prayer.*

Leader: "Contribute to the needs of the saints; extend hospitality to strangers."

People: *We will contribute to the needs of the saints and extend hospitality to strangers.*

Leader: "Bless those who persecute you; bless and do not curse them."

People: *We will bless those who persecute us; we will bless and not curse them.*

Leader: "Rejoice with those who rejoice, weep with those who weep."

People: *We will rejoice with those who rejoice and weep with those who weep.*

Leader: "Rejoice in the Lord always. I will say it again: Rejoice!"

People: *We will rejoice in the Lord always. We will say it again: Rejoice!*

(Rom. 12:1-2; Rom. 12:9-10a; 11-15 NRSV; Phil. 4:4 leader, not paraphrased; people, paraphrased)

6. REMEMBERING AND REJOICING

We will remember Your deeds, O Lord.

Yes, we will remember Your miracles of long ago.

They are constantly in our thoughts. We cannot stop thinking about them.

Your principles have been the music of our life throughout the years of our pilgrimage.

We will rejoice and be glad in Your lovingkindness, because You have seen our affliction.

Yes, Lord, You have known the troubles of our soul.

You have not given us over into the hand of the enemy.

You have set our feet in a large place.

You lifted us out of the pit of despair, out of the mud and the mire.

You set our feet on solid ground and steadied us as we walked along.

We will praise You, O Lord, with all our heart;

We will tell of all Your wonders.

We will be glad and rejoice in You.

We will sing praise to Your name, O Most High.

(Ps. 77:11; Ps. 77:12 NLT; Ps. 119:54 NLT; Ps. 31:7-8 NAS95; Ps. 40:2 NLT; Ps. 9:1-2, all paraphrased)

APPENDIX B:

Plans for a Small Group Study and Spiritual Retreat

Although *A Woman's Pilgrimage of Faith* was written for individuals, it can also be used by groups. The thirteen weeks of devotional studies make it ideal for a quarterly class schedule. The fourteenth week is a spiritual retreat that you will need to plan for and schedule.

This book is not recommended for use during a Sunday school hour because it is about how we respond to losses, the emotional pain and grief we experience, and what we're going through spiritually. Those who would find the book most helpful are women who have experienced or are now going through major trials and need to work on the grieving and the healing process both emotionally and spiritually.

For small groups it would be best to meet in a comfortable setting, with enough time set aside so that each person can share. You will need at least ninety minutes for a session, which allows for more personal sharing and prayer time. Serving light refreshments afterward gives women an added opportunity to share informally. Six women or fewer in each group would be ideal. If your group is large, you may want to break up into small groups for discussion after the leader speaks.

Confidentiality needs to be stressed because women will be sharing highly personal needs. They need to be able to trust each other and feel safe to share their painful experiences and spiritual struggles. When we're hurting, we're more fragile and vulnerable, so the leader needs to set a tone of affirmation, compassion, and support. (Some women may have such serious problems they will need encouragement to seek the help of a pastor and/or Christian counselor.)

A home may be more comfortable than a classroom. But if you meet in a classroom and the setting is less than ideal, you can make some adjustments. The class I taught met in the preschoolers' room. Every week I put the toys away and set up a portable screen to block off part of the play area. I decorated a small table with either a crocheted or lace cloth, lighted candles, flowers, or other simple decorations.

A week before the first meeting, make sure the women in the class have this book. Ask them to read and do the devotionals for Week One, "Storm-Tossed Faith." Then you will be able to begin group discussion right away.

Leader Preparation

Plan to cover the weekly chapters in one or two class sessions. You'll have enough time to cover the introductory chapter and seven devotionals if you take two sessions, extending the class to twenty-six weeks. If you choose to cover the entire chapter and devotionals during one class session, it will help to decide which statements or questions from "Practicing the Spiritual Life" you will use for discussion.

As you read over the chapter and do the devotions each week, highlight or underline the main points and spiritual applications. Make note of the ways the Lord ministers to you as you read the chapter and do the devotions. Then share with the class personal examples of how the Lord spoke to your heart and helped you.

Be transparent about your own personal and spiritual struggles. If you present yourself as the perfect Christian, class members will find it hard to be open and vulnerable.

Prayer is an essential part of your preparation. At the first class, pass out small index cards, giving two to each woman. Ask the women to write the same prayer request on both cards. The leader keeps one card and asks the women to find a partner with whom they can exchange their other prayer request card. Encourage the women to pray for each other throughout the week.

During prayer time, the women can refer to the requests on the card as they're praying. It works best to have two or three women pray together, because it is more personal and private. If the group is large, taking everyone's requests can be too time consuming, and many women won't share their needs in front of the others. Some women won't feel comfortable praying aloud. Pair those who are uncomfortable praying aloud with someone who can pray for both of them. It's important for the leader to use the prayer request cards to remember the women and to follow up by asking them about their requests.

Small Group Guidelines

Though some women may not feel comfortable writing in a published book, encourage them to do so. They may also want to use notebook paper or a journal to write additional comments, verses, or spiritual insights (see the Introduction for more guidelines).

Have the women sit in a circle, semicircle, or around a table. This makes the class more personal and facilitates discussion. Women who are hard of hearing read lips and facial expressions to help them hear better, so they especially need to see who is speaking.

If the class is large, divide it into groups of four to six women. Either choose discussion leaders or ask the groups to choose their own. Many women feel more comfortable sharing when there are fewer members. This also allows them to participate more, and they can get to know each other in a more personal way.

Encourage the women to read the chapter and complete the devotionals prior to each session. Lack of preparation limits the discussion, because fewer women are ready to share. The more women who prepare, the greater the benefit for the entire group and for themselves as well.

Encourage the women to highlight or underline passages in the text that were especially meaningful and reflect on these. Ask them to return to class ready to share spiritual insights and/or questions. This will make the class more interesting and will be an incentive for the other members.

Class Session Plans

For the first session, go over the Introduction with the women to give them an overview of the book and help them know what to expect. The weekly title page has a Scripture passage that the women may memorize. This is difficult for some women, so be careful not to embarrass those who don't learn the verses. Other women may want to memorize some of the verses but not all of them.

This devotional study is for women in different stages of spiritual growth. Encourage those who are embarrassed because they don't have devotions or who feel guilty about the amount of time they spend with the Lord. Others may try to have devotions but can't keep their thoughts focused, or they may come away feeling dry or dissatisfied. This class is for all seekers who desire to find healing and grow in their faith.

Here is a format that you may want to follow for the class:

Open class with prayer and move right into the study, or begin with a hymn or worship songs. If you don't have someone who can play the piano or guitar, sing along with cassette tapes or sing without an instrument.

If you have one small group, discuss together the highlights of the chapter and the questions or statements from "Practicing the Spiritual Life." If the class is large, briefly share highlights from the introductory chapter, giving personal illustrations from your own spiritual pilgrimage. Then the class can go to their small groups to discuss the devotionals.

If time permits, have refreshments after the session. This will also give some women the opportunity to ask you questions that they didn't feel comfortable discussing with their group. If there are group leaders, ask them to be available to the women in their groups during this time.

Many women are busy and work long hours, so it is important to begin and end on time. Those who want to stay afterward will, and those who need to leave will feel free to go.

Group Discussion Guidelines

Open discussion and group participation are the best methods for using this book. Women remember more of what they do and say, so keep lectures to a minimum. Be a facilitator who guides the discussion and keeps the class on track and on schedule.

Be relaxed, and the class will feel more at ease. This doesn't mean that the class is unstructured. Maintain an informal friendly manner while guiding the discussion in an orderly way.

Involve as many women as possible. You may want to go around the group, asking each member to answer different questions or contribute a comment. Women who don't feel comfortable entering into the discussion may be willing to read Scripture aloud.

Ask the group to share personal examples of what they learned in the devotional study or of how God has been working in their lives and changing them. The more the women see that the Lord can change people's lives, the more enthusiastic they may be about growing in their faith.

Some women feel uncomfortable answering the personal questions about their spiritual life. Others will gladly volunteer. Respect their comfort level.

The group will gain more from the class if you try to keep the discussion balanced. If the women go off on tangents, bring the discussion back to the main topic as quickly as possible.

Keep more vocal members from dominating the group. When a person keeps talking without pausing, you may have to interrupt. You might say something like this, "Excuse me, we appreciate what you have to say, but we need to give others an opportunity to share." Then ask another person to contribute an answer.

Everyone is in a different place spiritually. Some of the women will be mature; others will be new believers. Some will be committed to growing in their faith; others will have little desire to grow. Some women have been Christians for many years but have not grown in their faith. They may be defensive, embarrassed, or unaware of their spiritual condition. Still others may be angry, bitter, and/or rebellious due to painful experiences.

Most women feel inferior around someone who seems to have all the correct answers and can quote the right verse for every difficulty. Some women may spiritualize their problems and appear to handle their lives in a perfect manner no matter how many trials they face. This causes others to feel they are being judged or that they do not measure up to the standards of perfect Christians.

Set an open, accepting tone by constantly affirming those who feel they aren't as spiritual as others. Be gracious and kind to those who are hurting deeply and/or questioning their faith. Be patient and loving with those who have bitter attitudes. Pray for the transforming power of the Holy Spirit to work in all of your lives.

We all need the assurance that our Lord loves us with a love that is beyond our comprehension. Because He loves us so much, He will always be available to support and strengthen us as we grow in Him, and we need to do the same for each other.

The Devotional Retreat

A retreat for spiritual renewal might also be called a silent retreat, because the women will be spending time alone with the Lord without talking to each other. During this time they will be using the Week Fourteen, "Remember and Rejoice," spiritual retreat guide and their Bibles.

You may want to begin the retreat with worship songs. Then silence is maintained until the early afternoon when the group gathers for the Remembrance Ceremony. Though the idea of being with others without speaking may seem difficult, the group will discover that this time alone with the Lord will be spiritually renewing.

When I first mentioned to the women in our class that we would be spending a day together without talking, they couldn't imagine that it would be possible. At the end of the retreat, however, they felt that the time had gone by too quickly and were already talking about having another one.

The women will need reassurance, because they will feel uncomfortable about not speaking to the others. A silent devotional retreat has an added dimension that you may miss when you have a retreat alone. You feel the prayers and the presence of Lord when many are gathered together. You feel spiritually strengthened and uplifted by the other women even though you aren't talking with them.

Group Retreat Plans

Choose a quiet, peaceful place for the retreat. We had a one-day retreat at a home with a lovely garden and pool. A small park was a block away. Some women sat by the pool, others in the front yard, while others went to the park. If you have a conference center nearby, you may be able to use their grounds for a day.

Set a day and time for the retreat. We had ours on a Saturday from 9:30 A.M. to 3:30 P.M. Depending on the desires of your group, you may want to start earlier and/or go later in the day.

Make a sign-up sheet for the women to help with setup and cleanup and to bring food and paper goods. Keep food simple and light; we had sand-wiches for lunch. We also had coffee, juice, sodas, muffins, and fresh fruit available throughout the day for snacks. For our afternoon fellowship time we had a light dessert.

We didn't have the morning snack or lunch together. Some women set up the snack while others laid out the food for lunch. Others took care of cleaning up. We maintained our time of silence during this time and until we met for worship and fellowship in the afternoon.

Have a closing Remembrance Ceremony and a fellowship time with a snack. Use the "Spiritual Retreat and Remembrance Ceremony Guide" on page 220 and the "Responsive Readings for Groups" on page 220 to plan your service.

The retreat guide, "Remember and Rejoice," would also work well for a weekend retreat. I have been on a private spiritual retreat at a center where we remained silent until the evening meal. At that time, we shared around the table and had an evening worship and prayer service. Sunday morning could include a time of silence followed by a worship service, Remembrance Ceremony, and Communion.

Our retreat was a spiritually renewing experience. For me, it was life-changing as I sat at Jesus' feet and felt His powerful presence in the love and prayers of my friends. The Lord sent me out from that time with a greater desire to serve Him.

It is my prayer that as you go forth to comfort, minister, and serve others that you may be filled with joyous praise as you watch with wonder the transforming work of the Lord in your life and the lives of others.

NOTES

WEEK ONE: STORM-TOSSED FAITH

1. Edith Schaeffer, *Affliction* (Old Tappan, N.J.: Fleming H.Revell, 1973), 79.
2. Gerald L. Sittser, *A Grace Disguised: How the Soul Grows Through Loss* (Grand Rapids: Zondervan Publishing House, 1996), 10.
3. Ibid.
4. Ibid., 9.

WEEK TWO: SHOCK AND DISBELIEF

1. Gerald L. Sittser, *A Grace Disguised: How the Soul Grows Through Loss* (Grand Rapids: Zondervan Publishing House, 1996), 18.
2. Catherine M. Sanders, *Surviving Grief . . . and Learning to Live Again* (New York: John Wiley & Sons, 1992), 42.
3. Charles F. Pfeiffer and Everett F. Harrison, eds., *The Wycliffe Bible Commentary* (Chicago: Moody Press, 1962), 983.
4. Francis I. Andersen, *Job* (Downers Grove, Ill.: InterVarsity Press, 1976), 96.
5. Judie Frank, "I'll Be There," copyright 1997. All rights reserved. Used by permission.

WEEK THREE: SHATTERED BY SORROW

1. Gerald L. Sittser, *A Grace Disguised: How the Soul Grows Through Loss* (Grand Rapids: Zondervan Publishing House, 1996), 18-19.
2. William A. Miller, *When Going to Pieces Holds You Together* (Minneapolis: Augsburg Publishing House, 1976), 18.
3. Nathan Kollar, *Songs of Suffering* (Minneapolis: Winston Press, 1982), 33-34.
4. Catherine M. Sanders, *Grief the Mourning After: Dealing with Adult Bereavement* (New York: John Wiley & Sons, 1989), 60.
5. Ibid., 9.
6. Miller, *When Going to Pieces*, 30.
7. Morrie Schwartz, *Letting Go: Morrie's Reflections on Living While Dying* (New York: Dell Publishing, 1996), 30.
8. Miller, *When Going to Pieces*, 49.
9. Judie Frank, "God Was Faithful," copyright 1998. All rights reserved. Used by permission.

WEEK FOUR: SECONDARY LOSSES

1. Therese A. Rando, *Grieving: How to Go on Living When Someone You Love Dies* (Lexington, Mass.: Lexington Books, 1988), 15.
2. Ibid., 13.
3. Elizabeth Harper Neeld, *Seven Choices: Taking the Steps to New Life After Losing Someone You Love* (New York: Clarkson N. Potter Publishers, 1990), 78.
4. Madame Jeanne Guyon, *The Book of Job* (Gardiner, Maine: Christian Books Publishing House, 1985), 47.
5. Mildred Tengbom, *Sometimes I Hurt: Reflections and Insights from the Book of Job* (Nashville: Thomas Nelson Publishers, 1980), 129-30.
6. Oswald Chambers, *Christian Discipline: Vol. 1, The Discipline of Suffering* (Fort Washington, Penn.: Christian Literature Crusade, 1936), 62-63.
7. Oswald Chambers, *Still Higher for His Highest* (Fort Washington, Penn.: Christian Literature Crusade, 1970), 76.
8. Matthew Henry, *Commentary on the Whole Bible* (Grand Rapids: Zondervan Publishing House, 1961), 1289.
9. Ibid.

10. Madame Jeanne Guyon, *Experiencing the Depths of Jesus Christ* (Auburn, Maine: Christian Books Publishing House, 1975), 37.
11. Ibid., 39.
12. Oswald Chambers, *Not Knowing Whither* (Fort Washington, Penn.: Christian Literature Crusade, 1934), 105.
13. Henry, *Commentary*, 1289.
14. Oswald Chambers, *Daily Thoughts for Disciples* (Grand Rapids: Zondervan Publishing House, 1976), May 16, 99.
15. Ibid., 66.
16. Oswald Chambers, *My Utmost for His Highest: An Updated Edition in Today's Language* (Grand Rapids: Discovery House Publishers, 1992), June 26.

WEEK FIVE: DEALING WITH DENIAL

1. Peter C. McDonald, "Grieving: A Healing Process" (Center City, Minn.: Hazelden Educational Materials, 1985), 6.
2. Nathan Kollar, *Songs of Suffering* (Minneapolis: Winston Press, 1982), 22.
3. Joseph Bayly, *The View from a Hearse: A Christian View of Death* (Elgin, Ill.: David C. Cook Publishing, 1969), 68.
4. Oswald Chambers, *My Utmost for His Highest: An Updated Edition in Today's Language* (Grand Rapids: Discovery House Publishers, 1992), May 15.
5. Ibid.
6. Ibid., November 5.
7. Oswald Chambers, *Still Higher for His Highest* (Fort Washington, Penn.: Christian Literature Crusade, 1970), 34.
8. Ibid.

WEEK SIX: ANGER AND BITTERNESS

1. Elizabeth Harper Neeld, *Seven Choices: Taking the Steps to New Life After Losing Someone You Love* (New York: Clarkson N. Potter, Publishers, 1990), 129-30.
2. Elisabeth Kübler-Ross, *On Death and Dying* (New York: Macmillan Publishing, 1969), 50.
3. Neeld, *Seven Choices*, 39.
4. Gerald L. Sittser, *A Grace Disguised: How the Soul Grows Through Loss* (Grand Rapids: Zondervan Publishing House, 1996), 87.
5. Ibid., 88.
6. Mark P. Cosgrove, *Counseling for Anger* (Dallas: Word Publishing, 1988), 81.
7. Ibid., 79.
8. Ibid., 83.
9. Ibid.
10. Oswald Chambers, *My Utmost for His Highest: An Updated Edition in Today's Language* (Grand Rapids: Discovery House Publishers, 1992), May 11.
11. Judie Frank, "Give Me Peace Anew," copyright 1997. All rights reserved. Used by permission.

WEEK SEVEN: ANXIETY AND FEAR

1. Catherine M. Sanders, *Surviving Grief . . . and Learning to Live Again* (New York: John Wiley & Sons, 1992), 65-66.
2. Men and Women in Anonymous Programs, *Living Recovery: Inspirational Moments for 12-Step Living* (New York: Ballantine Books, 1990), 103.
3. Les Troyer, "The Faith and Concern of a Child," *In Other Words*, vol. 4, no. 8, Wycliffe Bible Translators, Nov. 1978, 8.
4. Men and Women, *Living Recovery*, 96.
5. Edith Schaeffer, *Affliction* (Old Tappan, N.J.: Fleming H. Revell Company, 1973), 75.
6. Neil T. Anderson, *Walking in the Light* (Nashville: Thomas Nelson Publishers, 1992), 62.

7. Neil T. Anderson, *The Bondage Breaker* (Eugene, Ore.: Harvest House Publishers, 1960), 84.
8. Schaeffer, *Affliction*, 93.
9. Anderson, *Walking in the Light*, 63.
10. Schaeffer, *Affliction*, 75.
11. Anderson, *Walking in the Light*, 63.

WEEK EIGHT: BARGAINING AND DEPRESSION

1. Elisabeth Kübler-Ross, *On Death and Dying* (New York: Macmillan Publishing, 1969), 83-84.
2. Peter C. McDonald, "Grieving: A Healing Process" (Center City, Minn.: Hazelden, 1985), 9.
3. Ibid.
4. Kübler-Ross, *On Death*, 84.
5. Edith Schaeffer, *Affliction* (Old Tappan, N.J.: Fleming H. Revell Company, 1973), 91-92.
6. Kübler-Ross, *On Death*, 84.
7. Ibid., 82.
8. Elizabeth Harper Neeld, *Seven Choices: Taking the Steps to New Life After Losing Someone You Love* (New York: Clarkson N. Potter, Publishers, 1990), 85.
9. Ibid.
10. Archibald D. Hart, *Counseling the Depressed* (Dallas: Word Publishing, 1987), 23, 25, 27, 28-29.
11. Ibid., 24, 29.
12. Catherine M. Sanders, *Surviving Grief . . . and Learning to Live Again* (New York: John Wiley & Sons, 1992), 74.
13. Oswald Chambers, *Daily Thoughts for Disciples* (Grand Rapids: Zondervan Publishing House, 1976), December 10, 229.
14. Roy W. Fairchild, *Finding Hope Again: A Pastor's Guide to Counseling Depressed Persons* (San Francisco: Harper & Row, Publishers, 1980), 51.
15. Ibid., 50-51.
16. Oswald Chambers, *My Utmost for His Highest: An Updated Edition in Today's Language* (Grand Rapids: Discovery House Publishers, 1992), September 20.
17. Fairchild, *Finding Hope Again*, 52.
18. Matthew Henry, *Commentary on the Whole Bible* (Grand Rapids: Zondervan Publishing House, 1961), 1764.
19. Fairchild, *Finding Hope Again*, 51.
20. Judie Frank, "Lord, You Are My Hope," copyright 1998. All rights reserved. Used by permission.

WEEK NINE: SECURE IN GOD'S FORGIVENESS

1. Craig Nimmo and Robert Griffin, "Failure?" *In Other Words*, Wycliffe Bible Translators, February 1979, 1-3.
2. Elizabeth Harper Neeld, *Seven Choices: Taking the Steps to New Life After Losing Someone You Love* (New York: Clarkson N. Potter, Publishers, 1990), 38-39.
3. Larry K. Weeden, *Feeling Guilty, Finding Grace: If I'm Forgiven, Why Do I Feel So Bad?* (Ann Arbor: Servant Publications, 1998), 38.
4. Ibid., 38, 77.
5. Ibid., 39.
6. Ibid., 89-90.
7. Ibid., 148.
8. Ibid., 91.
9. Ibid., 92, 93, 94.
10. Ibid., 125.
11. Ibid.

WEEK TEN: SPIRITUAL TURNING POINT

1. Gerald L. Sittser, *A Grace Disguised: How the Soul Grows Through Loss* (Grand Rapids: Zondervan Publishing House, 1996), 70.
2. Ibid., 71.
3. Ibid., 74.
4. Tim Hansel, *You Gotta Keep Dancin'* (Elgin, Ill.: David C. Cook Publishing, Co., 1985), 94.
5. Ibid., 122.
6. Ibid., 96, 121-122.
7. Sittser, *Grace Disguised*, 79.
8. Catherine M. Sanders, *Surviving Grief. . . and Learning to Live Again* (New York: John Wiley & Sons, 1992), 89.
9. Elizabeth Harper Neeld, *Seven Choices: Taking the Steps to New Life After Losing Someone You Love* (New York: Clarkson N. Potter, Publishers, 1990), 152.
10. Morrie Schwartz, *Letting Go: Morrie's Reflections on Living While Dying* (New York: Dell Publishing, 1996), 39.
11. Sittser, *Grace Disguised*, 78.
12. Neeld, *Seven Choices*, 153.
13. Victor E. Frankl, *Man's Search for Meaning* (New York: Simon and Schuster, 1970), 65-66.
14. Judie Frank, "Letting Go of Yesterday," copyright 1998. All rights reserved. Used by permission.

WEEK ELEVEN: SEARCH FOR SPIRITUAL MEANING

1. Edith Schaeffer, *Affliction* (Old Tappan, N.J.: Fleming H. Revell Company, 1973), 92.
2. Charles E. Cowman, Mrs., *Streams in the Desert* (Grand Rapids: Zondervan Publishing House, 1965), March 22, 91.
3. Oswald Chambers, *Christian Discipline, Vol. 1, The Discipline of Suffering* (Fort Washington, Penn.: Christian Literature Crusade, 1936), 61.
4. Philip Yancey, *Disappointment with God: Three Questions No One Asks Aloud* (New York: Harper Paperbacks, 1988), 294.
5. Gerald L. Sittser, *A Grace Disguised: How the Soul Grows Through Loss* (Grand Rapids: Zondervan Publishing House, 1996), 138.
6. Ibid., 141-42, 136.
7. Tim Hansel, *You Gotta Keep Dancin'* (Elgin, Ill.: David C. Cook Publishing Co., 1985), 96.
8. Victor E. Frankl, *Man's Search for Meaning* (New York: Simon and Schuster, 1970), 116.
9. Ibid., 67.
10. Morrie Schwartz, *Letting Go: Morrie's Reflections on Living While Dying* (New York: Dell Publishing, 1996), 64.
11. Catherine M. Sanders, *Surviving Grief. . . and Learning to Live Again* (New York: John Wiley & Sons, 1992), 98-99.
12. Frankl, *Man's Search*, 99, 110.
13. Sittser, *Grace Disguised*, 9-10.
14. Charles Stanley, *The Blessing of Brokenness: Why God Allows Us to Go Through Hard Times* (Grand Rapids: Zondervan Publishing House, 1997), 61.
15. Frankl, *Man's Search*, 35.
16. Sittser, *Grace Disguised*, 142-43.
17. Charles Hodge, *Romans* (Wheaton: Crossway Books, 1993), 261.
18. Oswald Chambers, *Still Higher for His Highest* (Fort Washington, Penn.: Christian Literature Crusade, 1970), 122.
19. Oswald Chambers, *My Utmost for His Highest: An Updated Edition in Today's Language* (Grand Rapids: Discovery House Publishers, 1992), March 7.

20. Matthew Henry, *Commentary on the Whole Bible* (Grand Rapids: Zondervan Publishing House, 1962), 1775.
21. Ibid., 1566.
22. Hodge, *Romans*, 265.
23. Oswald Chambers, *The Love of God: An Intimate Look at the Father-Heart of God* (Grand Rapids: Discovery House Publishers, 1988), 12.
24. Edith Schaeffer, *Affliction*, (Old Tappan: Fleming H. Revell Company, 1973), 88-89.
25. Chambers, *Love of God*, 20.
26. Judie Frank, "Jesus Loves Me," copyright 1998. All rights reserved. Used by permission.

WEEK TWELVE: RENEWED FAITH

1. G. Campbell Morgan, *The Answers of Jesus to Job* (Grand Rapids: Baker Book House, 1973), 47.
2. Peter Kreeft, *Making Sense Out of Suffering* (Ann Arbor: Servant Books, 1986), 133.
3. Ibid., 138.
4. Ibid.
5. Oswald Chambers, *Baffled to Fight Better* (Fort Washington, Penn.: Christian Literature Crusade, 1931), 68.
6. Morgan, *Answers of Jesus*, 44.
7. Steven J. Lawson, *When All Hell Breaks Loose, You May Be Doing Something Right: Surprising Insights from the Life of Job* (Colorado Springs: Navpress, 1993), 146.
8. Edith Schaeffer, *Affliction* (Old Tappan, N.J.: Fleming H. Revell Company, 1973), 80, 73.
9. Oswald Chambers, *Conformed to His Image* (Fort Washington, Penn.: Christian Literature Crusade, 1950), 112.
10. Schaeffer, *Affliction*, 79
11. Ibid., 73.
12. Ibid., 75.
13. Charles E. Cowman, Mrs., *Streams in the Desert* (Grand Rapids: Zondervan Publishing House, 1965), April 3, 104.

WEEK THIRTEEN: SERVE WITH COMPASSION

1. Charles E. Cowman, Mrs., *Streams in the Desert* (Grand Rapids: Zondervan Publishing House, 1965), September 6, 261.
2. Ibid., March 22, 91.
3. Robert L. Hunter, *Helping When It Hurts: A Practical Guide to Helping Relationships* (Philadelphia: Fortress Press, 1985), 20.
4. Hugh Smith, "Caring for the Widowed," *PrimeTimer*, (Summer 1998), 3.
5. Judie Frank, "The Phone Call," copyright 1998. All rights reserved. Used by permission.

INDEX

Discover the joy in the journey
As you travel the path with Him

You already know from experience that things aren't always what they could be, especially in the spiritual sense. That your "quiet time" with God isn't necessarily "quality time." But within your spirit you know that it can be different. That you can come away from devotions feeling renewed and refreshed.

Between the creative devotional ideas, the daily Scripture reading and study, and the application questions, *A Woman's Walk with God* strikes an excellent balance between doctrine and practice. It's exactly what you need to fashion the kind of spiritual life you've longed for: one that is personal, consistent, and a continuous source of refreshment.

Just say "Yes, Lord,"
And let the wondrous journey begin

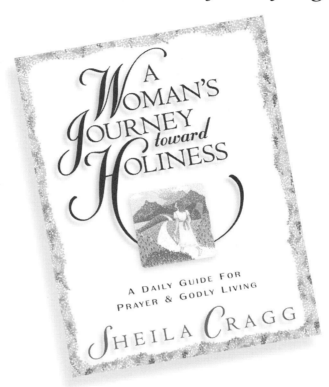

A WOMAN'S JOURNEY toward HOLINESS

A DAILY GUIDE FOR PRAYER & GODLY LIVING

SHEILA CRAGG

God has said, "Be ye holy; for I am holy." Your journey to fulfill His call begins with two words you'll never regret: "Yes, Lord."

Step by step as you surrender every part of your life to Him, you open the door to a richer relationship with Christ. *A Woman's Journey Toward Holiness* is designed to begin wherever you are in your spiritual walk and remove the obstacles you face along the way. The daily Scripture readings, reflective questions, and guided prayers will lead you farther and deeper into the Savior's heart and mind as your own heart, mind, and passions are transformed. And you will never be the same.